INTERACTIVE WHITEBOARD ACTIVITIES

D1515092

Math
LESSONS FOR THE SMART BOARD™

Motivating, Interactive Lessons That Teach Key Math Skills

SCHOLASTIC

New York ○ Toronto ○ London ○ Auckland ○ Sydney
New Delhi ○ Mexico City ○ Hong Kong ○ Buenos Aires

Teaching *Resources*

Author: Ann Montague-Smith
Illustrators: Jim Peacock, Jenny Tulip, Theresa Tibbetts
Editor: Maria L. Chang
Cover design: Brian LaRossa
Interior design: Grafica Inc.

CD-ROM developed in association with Q & D Multimedia

Special thanks to Robin Hunt and Melissa Rugless of Scholastic Ltd.

SMART Board™ and Notebook™ are registered trademarks of SMART Technologies Inc.
Microsoft Office, Word, and Excel are either registered trademarks or trademarks of Microsoft Corporation in the United States and/or other countries.

All Flash activities designed and developed by Q & D Multimedia.

Interactive Teaching Programs (developed by the Primary National Strategy) © Crown copyright.

ISBN: 978-0-545-29041-8

3 4 5 6 7 8 9 10   40   18 17 16 15 14 13 12

Contents

Introduction

Interactive whiteboards are fast becoming the must-have resource in today's classroom as they allow teachers to facilitate children's learning in ways that were inconceivable a few years ago. The appropriate use of interactive whiteboards, whether used daily in the classroom or once a week in a computer lab, encourages active participation in lessons and increases students' determination to succeed. Interactive whiteboards make it easier for teachers to bring subjects across the curriculum to life in new and exciting ways.

What can an interactive whiteboard offer?

For teachers, an interactive whiteboard allows them to do the same things they can on an ordinary whiteboard, such as drawing, writing, and erasing. However, the interactive whiteboard also offers many other possibilities, such as:

- saving any work created during a lesson;
- preparing as many pages as necessary;
- displaying any page within the Notebook™ file to review teaching and learning;
- adding scanned examples of children's work to a Notebook file;
- changing colors of shapes and backgrounds instantly;
- using simple templates and grids;
- linking Notebook files to spreadsheets, Web sites, and presentations.

Using an interactive whiteboard in the simple ways outlined above can enrich teaching and learning in a classroom, but that is only the beginning of the whiteboard's potential to educate and inspire.

For students, the interactive whiteboard provides the opportunity to share learning experiences, as lessons can be delivered with sound, still and moving images, and Web sites. Interactive whiteboards can be used to cater to the needs of all learning styles:

- Kinesthetic learners benefit from being able to physically manipulate images.
- Visual learners benefit from being able to watch videos, look at photographs, and see images being manipulated.
- Auditory learners benefit from being able to access audio resources, such as voice recordings and sound effects.

With a little preparation, all of these resource types could be integrated into one lesson—a feat that would have been almost impossible before the advent of the interactive whiteboard!

Access to an interactive whiteboard

In schools where students have limited access to an interactive whiteboard, carefully planned lessons will help students get the most benefit from it during the times they can use it. As teachers become familiar with the interactive whiteboard, they will learn when to use it and, equally important, when not to use it!

Where permanent access to an interactive whiteboard is available, it is important to plan the use of the board effectively. It should be used only in ways that will enhance or extend teaching and learning. Children still need to gain practical, firsthand experience of many things. Some experiences cannot be recreated on an interactive whiteboard, but others cannot be had without it. *Math Lessons for the SMART Board*™ offers both teachers and learners the most accessible and creative uses of this most valuable resource.

About the book

Adapted from Scholastic UK's best-selling 100 SMART Board™ Lessons series, *Math Lessons for the SMART Board* is designed to reflect best practice in using interactive whiteboards. It is also designed to support all teachers in using this valuable tool by providing lessons and other resources that can be used on the SMART Board with little or no preparation. These inspirational lessons meet the Common Core State Standards for Mathematics and the National Council of Teachers of Mathematics (NCTM) Standards and are perfect for all levels of experience.

This book is divided into four chapters. Each chapter contains lessons covering:

- Number & Operations
- Algebra Readiness
- Measurement & Data Analysis
- Geometry

Mini-Lessons

The mini-lessons have a consistent structure that includes:

- a **Getting Started** activity;
- a step-by-step **Mini-Lesson** plan;
- an **Independent Work** activity; and
- a **Wrap-Up** activity to round up the teaching and learning and identify any assessment opportunities.

Each mini-lesson identifies any resources required (including Notebook files that are provided on the CD-ROM, as well as reproducible activity pages) and lists the whiteboard tools that could be used in the mini-lesson.

The reproducible activity sheets toward the back of the book support the mini-lessons. These sheets provide opportunities for group or individual work to be completed away from the board, while linking to the context of the whiteboard lesson. They also provide opportunities for whole-class discussions in which children present their work.

What's on the CD-ROM?

The accompanying CD-ROM provides an extensive bank of Notebook files designed for use with the SMART Board. These support, and are supported by, the mini-lessons in this book. They can be annotated and saved for reference or for use with subsequent lessons; they can also be printed out. In addition to texts and images, a selection of Notebook files include the following types of files:

- **Embedded interactive files**: These include specially commissioned interactive files that will open in a new browser window within the Notebook environment.

- **Embedded audio files**: Some Notebook files contain buttons that play sounds.

- **"Build Your Own" file**: This contains a blank Notebook page with a bank of selected images and interactive tools from the Gallery, as well as specially commissioned images. You can use this to help build your own Notebook files.

The Notebook files

All of the Notebook files have a consistent structure as follows:

- **Title and objectives page**—Use this page to highlight the focus of the mini-lesson. You might also wish to refer to this page at certain times throughout the lesson or at the end of the lesson to assess whether the learning objective was achieved.

- **Getting Started activity**—This sets the context of the lesson and usually provides some key questions or learning points that will be addressed through the main activities.

- **Main activities**—These activities offer independent, collaborative group, or whole-class work. The activities draw on the full scope of Notebook software and the associated tools, as well as on the SMART Board tools. "What to Do" boxes are also included in many of the prepared Notebook files. These appear as tabs in the top right-hand corner of the screen. To access these notes, simply pull out the tabs to reveal planning information, additional support, and key learning points.

- **Wrap-Up**—A whole-class activity or summary page is designed to review work done both at the board and away from the board. In many lessons, children are encouraged to present their work.

How to Use the CD-ROM

Setting up your screen for optimal use

It is best to view the Notebook pages at a screen display setting of 1280 x 1024 pixels. To alter the screen display, select Settings, then Control Panel from the Start menu. Next, double-click on the Display icon, then click on the Settings tab. Finally, adjust the Screen Area scroll bar to 1280 x 1024 pixels. Click on OK. (On the Mac, click on the apple icon and select System Preferences. Then click on Displays and select 1280 x 1024.)

If you prefer to use a screen display setting of 800 x 600 pixels, ensure that your Notebook view is set to "Page Width." To alter the view, launch Notebook and click on View. Go to Zoom and select the "Page Width" setting. If you use a screen display setting of 800 x 600 pixels, text in the prepared Notebook files may appear larger when you edit it on screen.

Getting started

The program should run automatically when you insert the CD-ROM into your CD drive. If it does not, use My Computer to browse to the contents of the CD-ROM and click on the Scholastic icon. (On the Mac, click on the Scholastic icon to start the program.)

Main menu

The Main menu divides the Notebook files by topic: Number & Operations; Algebra Readiness; Measurement & Data Analysis; and Geometry. Clicking on the appropriate button for any of these options will take you to a separate Lessons menu. (See below for further information.) The "Build Your Own" file is also accessed through the Main menu.

Individual Notebook files or pages can be located using the search facility by keying in words (or part of words) from the resource titles in the Search box. Press Go to begin the search. This will bring up a list of the titles that match your search.

Lessons menu

Each Lessons menu lists all of the prepared Notebook files for each chapter of the book. Click on the buttons to open the Notebook files. Click on Main menu button to return to the Main menu screen. (To alternate between the menus on the CD-ROM and other open applications, hold down the Alt key and press the Tab key to switch to the desired application.)

"Build Your Own" file

Click on this button to open a blank Notebook page and a collection of Gallery objects, which will be saved automatically into the My Content folder in the Gallery. You only need to click on this button the first time you wish to access the "Build Your Own" file, as the Gallery objects will remain in the My Content folder on the computer on which the file was opened. To use the facility again, simply open a blank Notebook page and access the images and interactive resources from the same folder under My Content. If you are using the CD-ROM on a different computer, you will need to click on the "Build Your Own" button again.

Safety note: Avoid looking directly at the projector beam as it is potentially damaging to the eyes, and never leave children unsupervised when using the interactive whiteboard.

Connections to the Math Standards

The mini-lessons and activities in this book meet the following Common Core State Standards for Mathematics and the National Council of Teachers of Mathematics (NCTM) Standards:

	COMMON CORE STATE STANDARDS	NCTM STANDARDS
NUMBER & OPERATIONS		
Zero	**K.CC.4:** Understand the relationship between numbers and quantities. **K.CC.5:** Count to answer "how many?" questions about as many as 10 things in a scattered configuration. **K.OA.2:** Solve addition and subtraction word problems, and add and subtract within 10, e.g., by using objects or drawings to represent the problem.	• Count with understanding and recognize "how many" in sets of object • Connect number words and numerals to the quantities they represent, using various physical models and representations. • Understand the effects of adding and subtracting whole numbers.
Counting & Estimating; Reading Numerals; How Many?	**K.CC.4:** Understand the relationship between numbers and quantities. **K.CC.5:** Count to answer "how many?" questions about as many as 10 things in a scattered configuration.	• Count with understanding and recognize "how many" in sets of object • Connect number words and numerals to the quantities they represent, using various physical models and representations.
Writing Numerals	**K.CC.4:** Understand the relationship between numbers and quantities. **K.CC.5:** Count to answer "how many?" questions about as many as 10 things in a scattered configuration. **K.CC.3:** Write numerals from 0 to 20. Represent a number of objects with a written numeral 0–20.	• Count with understanding and recognize "how many" in sets of object • Connect number words and numerals to the quantities they represent, using various physical models and representations.
Comparing Quantities	**K.CC.5:** Count to answer "how many?" questions about as many as 10 things in a scattered configuration. **K.CC.6:** Identify whether the number of objects in one group is greater than, less than, or equal to the number of objects in another group, e.g., by using matching and counting strategies.	• Count with understanding and recognize "how many" in sets of object • Connect number words and numerals to the quantities they represent, using various physical models and representations.
Ordinal Numbers	**K.CC.7:** Compare two numbers between 1 and 10 presented as written numerals.	• Develop understanding of the relative position and magnitude of whole numbers and of ordinal and cardinal numbers and their connections.
Simple Word Problems	**K.CC.5:** Count to answer "how many?" questions about as many as 10 things in a scattered configuration. **K.CC.6:** Identify whether the number of objects in one group is greater than, less than, or equal to the number of objects in another group, e.g., by using matching and counting strategies. **K.OA.1:** Represent addition and subtraction with objects, fingers, mental images, drawings, sounds, acting out situations, verbal explanations, expressions, or equations. **K.OA.2:** Solve addition and subtraction word problems, and add and subtract within 10, e.g., by using objects or drawings to represent the problem.	• Count with understanding and recognize "how many" in sets of objects • Connect number words and numerals to the quantities they represent, using various physical models and representations. • Understand various meanings of addition and subtraction of whole numbers and the relationship between the two operations. • Understand the effects of adding and subtracting whole numbers.
Combining Two Groups; Combining Three Groups	**K.OA.1:** Represent addition and subtraction with objects, fingers, mental images, drawings, sounds, acting out situations, verbal explanations, expressions, or equations. **K.OA.2:** Solve addition and subtraction word problems, and add and subtract within 10, e.g., by using objects or drawings to represent the problem. **1.OA.5:** Relate counting to addition and subtraction.	• Understand various meanings of addition and subtraction of whole numbers and the relationship between the two operations. • Understand the effects of adding and subtracting whole numbers.
Counting On	**K.CC.2:** Count forward beginning for a given number within the known sequence (instead of having to begin at 1). **K.OA.1:** Represent addition and subtraction with objects, fingers, mental images, drawings, sounds, acting out situations, verbal explanations, expressions, or equations. **K.OA.2:** Solve addition and subtraction word problems, and add and subtract within 10, e.g., by using objects or drawings to represent the problem. **1.OA.5:** Relate counting to addition and subtraction. **1.NBT.1:** Count to 120, starting at any number less than 120.	• Understand various meanings of addition and subtraction of whole numbers and the relationship between the two operations. • Understand the effects of adding and subtracting whole numbers.
Doubling; Totals	**K.CC.2:** Count forward beginning for a given number within the known sequence (instead of having to begin at 1). **K.OA.1:** Represent addition and subtraction with objects, fingers, mental images, drawings, sounds, acting out situations, verbal explanations, expressions, or equations. **K.OA.2:** Solve addition and subtraction word problems, and add and subtract within 10, e.g., by using objects or drawings to represent the problem. **1.OA.5:** Relate counting to addition and subtraction.	• Understand various meanings of addition and subtraction of whole numbers and the relationship between the two operations. • Understand the effects of adding and subtracting whole numbers.

Breaking Down Numbers	**K.OA.3:** Decompose numbers less than or equal to 10 into pairs in more than one way and record each decomposition by a drawing or equation.	• Develop a sense of whole numbers and represent and use them in flexible ways, including relating, composing, and decomposing numbers.
Making Five	**K.OA.3:** Decompose numbers less than or equal to 10 into pairs in more than one way and record each decomposition by a drawing or equation. **K.OA.5:** Fluently add and subtract within 5.	• Develop a sense of whole numbers and represent and use them in flexible ways, including relating, composing, and decomposing numbers.
Taking Away	**K.OA.1:** Represent addition and subtraction with objects, fingers, mental images, drawings, sounds, acting out situations, verbal explanations, expressions, or equations. **1.OA.5:** Relate counting to addition and subtraction.	• Understand the effects of adding and subtracting whole numbers.
Counting Back; How Many Are Left?	**K.OA.2:** Solve addition and subtraction word problems, and add and subtract within 10, e.g., by using objects or drawings to represent the problem. **1.OA.5:** Relate counting to addition and subtraction.	• Understand various meanings of addition and subtraction of whole numbers and the relationship between the two operations. • Understand the effects of adding and subtracting whole numbers.
How Many More?	**K.CC.7:** Compare two numbers between 1 and 10 presented as written numerals. **K.OA.2:** Solve addition and subtraction word problems, and add and subtract within 10, e.g., by using objects or drawings to represent the problem. **1.OA.5:** Relate counting to addition and subtraction.	• Develop a sense of whole numbers and represent and use them in flexible ways, including relating, composing, and decomposing numbers. • Understand various meanings of addition and subtraction of whole numbers and the relationship between the two operations. • Understand the effects of adding and subtracting whole numbers.
Pick the Larger Number	**K.CC.2:** Count forward beginning for a given number within the known sequence (instead of having to begin at 1). **1.OA.5:** Relate counting to addition and subtraction.	• Understand various meanings of addition and subtraction of whole numbers and the relationship between the two operations. • Understand the effects of adding and subtracting whole numbers.
Solving Problems	**K.OA.2:** Solve addition and subtraction word problems, and add and subtract within 10, e.g., by using objects or drawings to represent the problem. **K.OA.3:** Decompose numbers less than or equal to 10 into pairs in more than one way and record each decomposition by a drawing or equation.	• Understand various meanings of addition and subtraction of whole numbers and the relationship between the two operations. • Understand the effects of adding and subtracting whole numbers.
Tens and Ones	**K.NBT.1:** Compose and decompose numbers from 11 to 19 into ten ones and some further ones and record each composition or decomposition by a drawing or equation; understand that these numbers are composed of ten ones and one, two, three, four, five, six, seven, eight, or nine ones. **1.OA.1:** Use addition and subtraction within 20 to solve word problems involving situations of adding to, taking from, putting together, taking apart, and comparing, with unknowns in all positions. **1.OA.2:** Solve word problems that call for addition of three whole numbers whose sum is less than or equal to 20.	• Use multiple models to develop initial understandings of place value and the base-ten number system.
Grouping for Easy Addition; Making Ten	**K.OA.2:** Solve addition and subtraction word problems, and add and subtract within 10, e.g., by using objects or drawings to represent the problem. **K.OA.3:** Decompose numbers less than or equal to 10 into pairs in more than one way and record each decomposition by a drawing or equation. **1.OA.6:** Add and subtract within 20, demonstrating fluency for addition and subtraction within 10. Use strategies such as making ten and decomposing a number leading to a ten.	• Develop a sense of whole numbers and represent and use them in flexible ways, including relating, composing, and decomposing numbers. • Understand various meanings of addition and subtraction of whole numbers and the relationship between the two operations. • Understand the effects of adding and subtracting whole numbers.
Coins	**K.OA.2:** Solve addition and subtraction word problems, and add and subtract within 10, e.g., by using objects or drawings to represent the problem.	• Understand the effects of adding and subtracting whole numbers.

ALGEBRA READINESS

What Comes Between?; Ordering Sets	**K.CC.6:** Identify whether the number of objects in one group is greater than, less than, or equal to the number of objects in another group, e.g., by using matching and counting strategies. **K.CC.7:** Compare two numbers between 1 and 10 presented as written numerals.	• Sort, classify, and order objects by size, number, and other properties.
Ordering Numbers	**K.CC.2:** Count forward beginning for a given number within the known sequence (instead of having to begin at 1). **K.CC.6:** Identify whether the number of objects in one group is greater than, less than, or equal to the number of objects in another group, e.g., by using matching and counting strategies. **K.CC.7:** Compare two numbers between 1 and 10 presented as written numerals.	• Sort, classify, and order objects by size, number, and other properties. • Develop understanding of the relative position and magnitude of whole numbers and of ordinal and cardinal numbers and their connections.
Number Order	**1.NBT.1:** Count to 120, starting at any number less than 120.	• Develop understanding of the relative position and magnitude of whole numbers and of ordinal and cardinal numbers and their connections.
Sorting	n/a	• Sort, classify, and order objects by size, number, and other properties.
Making Patterns	n/a	• Recognize, describe, and extend patterns such as sequences of sounds and shapes or simple numeric patterns and translate from one representation to another.
Extending Patterns	n/a	• Recognize, describe, and extend patterns such as sequences of sounds and shapes or simple numeric patterns and translate from one representation to another. • Analyze how both repeating and growing patterns are generated.

Find the Number	**K.OA.1:** Represent addition and subtraction with objects, fingers, mental images, drawings, sounds, acting out situations, verbal explanations, expressions, or equations. **K.OA.2:** Solve addition and subtraction word problems, and add and subtract within 10, e.g., by using objects or drawings to represent the problem. **1.OA.1:** Use addition and subtraction within 20 to solve word problems involving situations of adding to, taking from, putting together, taking apart, and comparing, with unknowns in all positions. **1.OA.3:** Apply properties of operations as strategies to add and subtract.	• Understand various meanings of addition and subtraction of whole numbers and the relationship between the two operations. • Understand the effects of adding and subtracting whole numbers. • Model situations that involve the addition and subtraction of whole numbers, using objects, pictures, and symbols.
What's Missing?	**K.CC.2:** Count forward beginning for a given number within the known sequence (instead of having to begin at 1). **1.OA.5:** Relate counting to addition and subtraction.	• Develop understanding of the relative position and magnitude of whole numbers and of ordinal and cardinal numbers and their connections.
Function Machine	**K.OA.2:** Solve addition and subtraction word problems, and add and subtract within 10, e.g., by using objects or drawings to represent the problem. **1.OA.6:** Add and subtract within 20, demonstrating fluency for addition and subtraction within 10. Use strategies such as creating equivalent but easier or known sums.	• Model situations that involve the addition and subtraction of whole numbers, using objects, pictures, and symbols.

MEASUREMENT & DATA ANALYSIS

Comparing Lengths; Units of Measurement	**K.MD.1:** Directly compare two objects with a measurable attribute in common, to see which object has "more of"/"less of" the attribute, and describe the difference. **1.MD.1:** Compare the lengths of two objects indirectly by using a third object. **1.MD.2:** Express the length of an object as a whole number of length units, by laying multiple copies of a shorter object (the length unit) end to end; understand that the length measurement of an object is the number of same-size length units that span it with no gaps or overlaps.	• Recognize the attributes of length, volume, weight, area, and time. • Compare and order objects according to these attributes. • Understand how to measure using nonstandard and standard units.
Ordering by Size	**K.MD.1:** Directly compare two objects with a measurable attribute in common, to see which object has "more of"/"less of" the attribute, and describe the difference.	• Recognize the attributes of length, volume, weight, area, and time. • Compare and order objects according to these attributes. • Understand how to measure using nonstandard and standard units.
Telling Time	**1.MD.3:** Tell and write time in hours and half-hours using analog clocks.	n/a
Collecting Data	**K.MD.3:** Classify objects into given categories; count the numbers of objects in each category and sort the categories by count. **1.MD.4:** Organize, represent, and interpret data with up to three categories; ask and answer questions about the total number of data points, how many in each category, and how many more or less are in one category than in another.	• Pose questions and gather data about themselves and their surroundings • Sort and classify objects according to their attributes and organize data about the objects.

GEOMETRY

2D Shapes	**K.G.2:** Correctly name shapes regardless of their orientations or overall size. **K.G.6:** Compose simple shapes to form larger shapes. **1.G.2:** Compose two-dimensional shapes or three-dimensional shapes to create a composite shape, and compose new shapes from the composite shape.	• Recognize, name, build, draw, compare, and sort two- and three-dimensional shapes. • Investigate and predict the results of putting together and taking apart two- and three-dimensional shapes.
More Shapes	**K.G.2:** Correctly name shapes regardless of their orientations or overall size. **K.G.3:** Identify shapes as two-dimensional or three-dimensional. **1.G.1:** Distinguish between defining attributes versus non-defining attributes. **1.G.2:** Compose two-dimensional shapes or three-dimensional shapes to create a composite shape, and compose new shapes from the composite shape.	• Recognize, name, build, draw, compare, and sort two- and three-dimensional shapes. • Investigate and predict the results of putting together and taking apart two- and three-dimensional shapes.
What's in a Shape?	**K.G.2:** Correctly name shapes regardless of their orientations or overall size. **K.G.3:** Identify shapes as two-dimensional or three-dimensional. **1.G.1:** Distinguish between defining attributes versus non-defining attributes.	• Recognize, name, build, draw, compare, and sort two- and three-dimensional shapes. • Investigate and predict the results of putting together and taking apart two- and three-dimensional shapes.
Making Models	**K.G.6:** Compose simple shapes to form larger shapes. **1.G.2:** Compose two-dimensional shapes or three-dimensional shapes to create a composite shape, and compose new shapes from the composite shape.	• Recognize, name, build, draw, compare, and sort two- and three-dimensional shapes. • Investigate and predict the results of putting together and taking apart two- and three-dimensional shapes.
Mazes	n/a	• Describe, name, and interpret relative positions in space and apply ideas about relative position. • Describe, name, and interpret direction and distance in navigating space and apply ideas about direction and distance.

Zero

Learning objectives

- Know that a group of things changes in quantity when something is added or taken away.
- Show an interest in number problems.
- Begin to use the vocabulary involved in adding and subtracting.

Resources

- "Zero" Notebook file
- "Counting Mat" (p. 56)
- "Ten in the Bed" (p. 57)
- 10 counting toys for each child

Whiteboard tools

- Pen tray
- Select tool
- Delete button

Getting Started

Open the "Zero" Notebook file and go to page 2. Tell the following story: *There were ten spots on the ladybug's back. His mother counted the spots.* (Count the spots together.) *The next day she counted the spots and this time there were only nine.* (Repeat, counting down by one each time.) *At last, the ladybug had no spots.* At each stage remove one spot from the ladybug's back by using the Delete button (or choosing the Delete option from the drop-down menu).

Mini-Lesson

1. Show the five stars on page 3 of the Notebook file and ask children to count them.

2. Remove one of the stars and count again. Repeat, counting each time until there are no stars left.

3. Introduce the word *zero*. Explain that the word means "none" or "nothing." Use the Delete button to reveal the word and definition.

4. Repeat the process using pages 4 and 5, counting down the different quantities on the board until zero is reached. (For page 5, drag the cupcakes into the cake box instead of removing them.)

5. Go to page 6 and press on the star to start playing the song "Ten in the Bed." Continue in this way, through pages 8 to 15, for the duration of the song. Invite children to hold up their fingers to show how many are left each time. Draw their attention to the numbers displayed as the song counts down from ten.

6. When the song ends (on page 15), ask children how many would be left in the bed if the last one were to fall out. Reveal the answer on page 16: *zero*.

Independent Work

Arrange for children to work in groups of four to six with an adult. Each child will need ten counting toys and a "Counting Mat" (p. 56). The adult should specify a number of objects to count out onto the counting mat, then say how many to remove, so that children experience zero in context. For example: *Put out six onto your counting mat. Now move away four. How many are left? Move away one . . . and one more. What is left now?*

Limit the number range to five or six for younger or less-confident learners. Encourage older or more-confident learners to say simple number sentences to describe the work, such as: *I put out six. Now I move away five. I move away one more. Now there is nothing left.*

Provide each child with a copy of "Ten in the Bed" (p. 57). Help children to repeat the counting rhyme with you, covering each person with a counter as they fall out of bed, one at a time!

Wrap-Up

Show the set of eight flowers on page 17 of the Notebook file. Invite a child to remove three of them, by selecting each and using the Delete button. Ask: *How many are there now?* Repeat this, asking children to remove a given quantity each time until there is nothing left.

Counting & Estimating

Learning objectives
- Estimate how many objects can be seen and check by counting.
- Count reliably up to ten everyday objects.

Resources
- "Counting & Estimating" Notebook file
- "Counting Mat" (p. 56)
- 10 counting toys for each pair of children
- transparent boxes and counting objects

Whiteboard tools
- Pen tray
- Select tool
- Screen Shade
- Delete button

Getting Started

Open the "Counting & Estimating" Notebook file and go to page 2. Explain that you will reveal a set of pictures on the SMART Board. Remove the circles to reveal the objects and ask children to count how many they can see by pointing. Invite children who are younger or less confident to come and point with you to help them develop this skill. Repeat for page 3. Check the quantities by marking them with a Pen from the Pen tray. Continue this activity over time for quantities up to ten, using pages 4 and 5 of the Notebook file.

Mini-Lesson

1. Explain to children that you will show them a set of images on the SMART Board for just a little while.

2. Display the set of three images on page 6 of the Notebook file for about five seconds. Then use the Screen Shade to hide the screen. Ask: *How many do you think there were?*

3. Reveal the set again, and invite children to count to check their estimates. Ask: *Did you make a good guess?*

4. Now select the objects and press the Delete button to show a different way of organizing them. Discuss whether it is easier to estimate and count the objects in this order.

5. Repeat this for other quantities (up to ten), using pages 7 to 15 of the Notebook file.

Independent Work

Have children work in pairs. Give each pair a "Counting Mat" (p. 56) and ten counting toys. Invite partners to take turns scattering a handful of toys onto the counting mat. Encourage their partner to say straight away how many they think there are, so that there is no time to count. Now ask children to check how many by counting, either by touch, move, and count, or by point and count (depending upon their skill level or counting experience). As children work, ask questions such as: *Did you make a good guess? Why did you think that there were five toys?*

Consider limiting the number range to below six for younger or less-confident learners, by providing them with larger counting toys so that they take fewer in a handful. For older or more-confident learners, decide whether to provide slightly smaller counting toys in order to increase the number range.

In your counting area, provide transparent boxes with different numbers of objects for children to explore. Provide extra counting objects and empty boxes and allow children to play freely with them.

Wrap-Up

Pages 16 to 20 of the Notebook file contain larger sets of eight to ten images. Continue as before, displaying the page for about five seconds before enabling the Screen Shade and asking children to make an estimate of how many items they saw. Now reveal the images again, this time asking children to count. Ask: *Did you make a good guess?* Use different strategies to check and count. For example, mark the items with a Pen from the Pen tray as they are counted, or position them in a neater arrangement.

Reading Numerals

Learning objectives
- Recognize numerals 1 to 5.
- Recognize numerals 1 to 9.

Resources
- "Reading Numerals" Notebook file
- sorting toys
- "Counting Mat" (p. 56)
- "Numerals" (p. 58), copied onto cardstock and cut out to make sets of cards (Decide on the range of numbers to provide for each group.)

Whiteboard tools
- Pen tray
- Select tool
- Delete button

Getting Started
Go to page 2 of the "Reading Numerals" Notebook file and draw attention to the toys. Ask children to count, by pointing, to find out how many toys there are. Invite children who find this skill difficult to come to the board and do this with you. Continue to pages 3 and 4 for other quantities between three and six. Drag the toys into the toy box, counting one at a time, to confirm the quantities.

Mini-Lesson
1. Display page 5 of the Notebook file and ask children to count by pointing at the images. Invite an individual to come to the SMART Board and use a Pen from the Pen tray to strike through the objects as children count them. Ask: *What was the last number that you said? So how many are there?*

2. Invite another child to use the Eraser from the Pen tray to rub over the first shape to reveal a number. Ask: *What number is this? Does this number match the number of objects?* Let the child rub over the remaining shapes until the matching number is found.

3. Repeat using the sets of images and numbers on pages 6 to 9.

4. If appropriate, continue with pages 10 to 12, which display sets of eight to ten objects. (You could also use these pages in a later session.)

5. Go to page 13. Use a Pen from the Pen tray to trace over the number on the page. Encourage children to read it. Ask them to hold up that number of fingers.

6. Repeat this using pages 14 to 17 to practice numbers one to five, and pages 18 to 23 for numbers zero to ten.

Independent Work
Arrange for children to work in groups of four. Provide each group with some counting toys and a set of number cards from "Numerals" (p. 58). Provide each child with a copy of the "Counting Mat" (p. 56). The number cards should be placed facedown. Invite children to take turns turning over a number card. All children should count out that quantity of toys onto their counting mats. After several turns, ask children to spread their number cards out on the table. Let them take turns placing some toys onto their mats, with the quantity matching one of the number cards. The other children must count the items and decide which number card matches the quantity. To start with, limit children to numbers up to six (younger or less-confident learners to four, and older or more-confident to ten).

Wrap-Up
Provide each child with a set of 1-to-6 number cards. Display page 24 of the Notebook file. Ask children to point and count. When you say *Show me*, they must hold up the number that matches the quantity counted. Use the Delete button to remove the box to reveal the number on the page for children to check their answers. Press on the number to hear a cheer to show that it is correct. Repeat for different quantities on pages 25 to 29.

How Many?

Learning objectives
- Begin to represent numbers using fingers, marks on paper, or pictures.
- Recognize numerals 1 to 9.

Resources
- "Reading Numerals" Notebook file
- "Recording How Many" (p. 59)
- "Numerals" (p. 58), copied onto cardstock and cut out to make sets of cards

Whiteboard tools
- Pen tray
- Select tool
- Delete button
- Gallery

Getting Started
Choose a set of images from pages 2 to 4 of the "Reading Numerals" Notebook file. Ask children to count by pointing. Check by counting together, and move each item to the toy box as it is counted so that it is clear what still needs to be counted. Repeat for a different quantity.

Mini-Lesson
1. Go to page 5 of the Notebook file. Ask children to count how many items are on the page by pointing.

2. After the set has been counted, invite a child to use the Eraser from the Pen tray to rub over the shapes on the page until they find the matching number. Use a Pen to draw a circle around the correct number.

3. Next, draw a mark over each object on the page. Ask children to count how many marks you made. Ask: *Are there the same number of marks as objects? So how many objects or marks are there?*

4. Repeat the activity, using pages 6 to 12, and gradually build up to counting ten objects in a set. Invite individual children to make the marks to correspond to how many are in the set.

5. Move on to page 13 and ask children to read the number (3). Make three marks on the page and encourage children to count them. Establish that the number of marks is the same as the number on the page.

6. Use pages 14 to 23 to reinforce this concept.

Independent Work
Provide each child with a copy of "Recording How Many" (p. 59). Explain that they must read the number and draw that number of marks. Alternatively, children may like to draw some small pictures to represent how many.

Ask an adult to work with younger or less-confident learners as a group. Provide them with an 11" x 17" enlargement of the activity sheet. Suggest that children count out some counting toys for each number before making marks to represent how many. Challenge older or more-confident learners to choose their own quantities of counting toys, recording how many they have by making marks of their own choice on the back of the sheet.

Wrap-Up
Provide some further counting-by-pointing practice, using pages 24 to 29 of the Notebook file. Choose individuals to come to the SMART Board to count and make marks to represent the number of objects in the set. Ask them to choose a number card to represent the quantity. Delete the box to reveal the number on the page. Ask: *How many marks are there? How many are in the set?* Agree that the quantities of images and marks match, and that the number represents how many. Repeat for other quantities. Use the Random Number Generator from the Gallery to generate some random numbers for children to count. Ask them to match the quantities to the correct number card.

Writing Numerals

Learning objectives

- Match number and quantity correctly.
- Begin to represent numbers using fingers, marks on paper, or pictures.
- Recognize numerals 1 to 9.

Resources

- "Writing Numerals" Notebook file
- "Count and Write the Numbers" (p. 60)
- "Numerals" (p. 58), copied onto cardstock and cut out to make sets of cards
- individual whiteboards and pens
- counting toys

Whiteboard tools

- Pen tray
- Select tool
- Delete button

Getting Started

Prepare sets of number cards provided on "Numerals" (p. 58). Invite six volunteers to each hold a number card from 1 to 6. Reveal a set of one to six objects from pages 2 to 7 of the "Writing Numerals" Notebook file. Invite children to count by pointing. Ask them to hold up the correct number card. Then delete the box to reveal the number on the page for them to check their answer. Press on the number to hear a cheer, indicating that children are correct. Repeat for other quantities between one and six.

Mini-Lesson

1. Go to page 8 of the Notebook file and explain that you will write a number on the SMART Board. Invite children to "write" the same number, in the air, with large arm movements.

2. Use the Eraser from the Pen tray to erase your writing and repeat for all the numbers one to six. Over time, extend to up to ten.

3. Reveal the set on page 9 of the Notebook file. Ask children to count the objects by pointing. Then write the number to match the quantity on the SMART Board. Ask children to write it in the air with you.

4. Repeat for other quantities and numbers on pages 10 to 13.

5. Return to page 8 and erase your writing. Provide children with individual whiteboards and pens. Ask them to write the number that you say on their whiteboards. Write it at the same time as they do, on page 8, to remind them how to form the number correctly.

6. Repeat for other numbers up to seven.

Independent Work

Ask children to work in pairs. Provide each child with a copy of "Count and Write the Numbers" (p. 60). Invite partners to take turns taking some counting toys and counting them. They should then write the number and draw the toys or make marks to represent how many.

Vary the number of counting toys to suit children's different abilities. Most children should have six toys; fewer for younger or less-confident learners, and up to ten for older or more-confident learners.

Wrap-Up

Using page 14 of the Notebook file, invite children from each ability group to use a Pen from the Pen tray (set to a thick setting) to draw a given quantity of marks. Encourage them to write the corresponding number.

Comparing Quantities

Learning objectives

- Begin to make comparisons between quantities.
- Compare two groups of objects, saying when they have the same number.
- Use language such as *more* or *less* to compare two numbers.

Resources

- "Comparing Quantities" Notebook file
- 20 counting toys and two set circles for each pair of children (You can create your own "set circles" by cutting 2-foot lengths of yarn, tying together the ends of each piece, and setting them like circles on a table.)

Whiteboard tools

- Pen tray
- Select tool
- Highlighter pen

Getting Started

Start with some counting-by-pointing practice. Invite between five and ten children to stand at the front of the class. Ask children to count by pointing to identify how many there are. Repeat for other quantities.

Mini-Lesson

1. Display the four-column staircase of squares on page 2 of the "Comparing Quantities" Notebook file. (There is a small space between the columns to avoid any confusion with rows.)

2. Ask children to look at each column in turn and to count how many squares there are by pointing.

3. Now point to the three- and four-square columns and ask: *Which has more? How many more?*

4. Repeat this for columns two and four and ask: *Which has fewer? How many fewer?*

5. Now invite a volunteer to come and make a bigger column of squares by dragging and dropping the squares from the circle to a new column next to the column of four squares. Count each square as it is dragged across. Ask: *How many squares does the new column have? How many more squares does it have than the four-square column?*

6. Go to page 3, which shows a pair of sets. Discuss the set circles and how these separate the two sets. Count each set. Ask: *Which has more? Which has fewer?* Challenge older or more-confident learners to say how many more or fewer there are.

7. Repeat this using the sets on pages 4 to 9.

Independent Work

Display page 10 of the Notebook file. Help children take turns dragging the blocks to make a staircase from one to five. Next, arrange for children to work in pairs. Provide each pair with 20 counting toys and two set circles. Ask partners to take turns putting two sets of toys into the set circles. Their partner must count each set and say which has more and which has fewer.

Provide fewer counting toys for younger or less-confident learners so that their quantity range is limited to no more than six in each set. Challenge older or more-confident learners to compare their two sets and to say how many more or fewer there are each time. As children work, ask questions such as: *Which has more/fewer? How many more/fewer? How do you know? How did you work that out?*

Wrap-Up

Use the 1-to-10 staircase on page 11 of the Notebook file for further practice in comparing quantities. Point to different columns and ask questions such as: *How many squares are in this column? How many more are there in this one? Are there more or fewer squares in this column?* Provide further practice of comparing sets by revisiting a selection of pages from 3 and 9. Note whether children understand the vocabulary *more* and *fewer*. Plan further work for those who are still unsure.

Ordinal Numbers

Learning objectives
- Use ordinal numbers in different contexts.
- Say and use number names in order in familiar contexts.

Resources
- "Ordinal Numbers" Notebook file
- "Which is First?" (p. 61)
- crayons
- counting toys

Whiteboard tools
- Pen tray
- Select tool

Getting Started

Count from one to ten together, keeping a brisk pace. Open the "Ordinal Numbers" Notebook file and go to page 2. Press on the image to watch the numbered procession of animals, counting together as the animals move across the screen. Look at the procession a second time, this time inviting children to say the numbers from one to ten in turn. If a child falters, pause the procession to allow them more time to focus on the number. Press Play to continue the procession.

Mini-Lesson

1. Go to page 3 of the Notebook file and press on the image to open the "Animal Parade" labeling activity. Look at the numbered animals around the edge. Point to the numbers, in any order, one at a time, and ask children to read the number.

2. Still using page 3, ask children to name the animals. Invite individuals to come to the board to drag and drop them into the correct number order. (Two of the animals have already been placed to start them off.)

3. Encourage the use of ordinal number as they work, by asking questions such as: *Which one is first? Is the elephant second?*

4. Go to page 4. Ask: *Which car is first? Which car is third?* and so on.

5. Let individual children have fun moving the cars around the page. Keep asking them to describe the order, using the appropriate language.

6. Repeat the activity, using the farm animals on page 5. Ask more searching questions, such as: *Which animal is between the first and third? Which is between the third and fifth? How many animals are between the second and fifth?*

7. Press on an animal to hear the sound that it makes.

Independent Work

Arrange for children to work in groups of four to six with an adult. Provide crayons and a copy of "Which is First?" (p. 61) for each child. Invite children to point to the first car and color it blue. Repeat this for each of the other cars in turn (the second in green and so on). Now invite children to point to specified cars: *Point to the fifth car. What color is the car between the third and fifth cars?*

Use counting toys (or beads on a lace) to support younger or less-confident learners. Challenge older or more-confident learners to put out ten different counting toys and repeat the activity using ordinal numbers up to *tenth*.

Wrap-Up

Go back to the animal procession on page 2 of the Notebook file and encourage children to say which animal is first, second, third, and so on. Check that they use and understand ordinal numbers (at this stage some children may just give the numbers, such as *one, two,* and *three*). Organize children into four teams to play the race game on page 6 as a fun way to conclude the session. Press on the button to view the rules of the game.

Simple Word Problems

Learning objectives
- Compare two groups of objects, saying when they have the same number.
- Say the number that is one more than a given number.
- Find one more or one less than a number from one to ten.

Resources
- "Simple Word Problems" Notebook file
- "Solve the Problems" (p. 62)
- counting toys
- drawing materials

Whiteboard tools
- Pen tray
- Select tool

Getting Started
Open the "Simple Word Problems" Notebook file and go to page 2. Encourage children to read aloud the numbers one to ten as you write them into the number track. Ask questions such as: *Which number is between one and three? Which numbers are between two and five?*

Mini-Lesson
1. Go to page 3 of the Notebook file and move four cars into one of the empty set circles. Ask children to count by pointing, and tell you how many cars there are.

2. Say: *There are four cars. Another car parks next to them* (drag one across). *How many cars are there now?* Agree that there are five. Now tell children that one of the cars has driven away (drag one away). Ask: *How many are left?*

3. Go to page 4 and drag six soccer balls into one of the set circles. Repeat the one more/one less questions for this set.

4. Repeat the activity one more time on page 5.

Independent Work
Arrange for children to work in groups of four to six with an adult. Each group will need a copy of "Solve the Problems" (p. 62). Ask the adult to discuss with children what each picture shows, and how many. The adult should pose a word problem, such as: *There are four rabbits in the wood. One more joins (or leaves) them. How many rabbits are there now?* Ask the adult to repeat this for each of the pictures.

Provide younger or less-confident learners with counting toys so that they can count out the appropriate quantity of toys, and add one more, or remove one, to reflect the word problem. Challenge older or more-confident learners to make up a word problem of their own for one more or one less. Invite them to draw suitable pictures for their problem.

Check these problems before the Wrap-Up, then scan their pictures and add them to page 6 of the Notebook file. (Upload scanned images by selecting Insert, then Picture File, and browsing to where you have saved the images.)

Wrap-Up
Display a picture made by one of the older or more-confident learners. Ask the child to explain the problem. Invite the other children to say the answer. Repeat this for some of the other problems that the older or more-confident learners have made up. Create a set of eight cars using page 2 of the Notebook file. Ask: *How many cars can you see?* Point to one and say: *This one drove away* (drag the car from the set and drop it). *How many are left?* Continue, this time moving one more car to join the others.

Combining Two Groups

Learning objectives

- Know that a group of things changes in quantity when something is added or taken away.
- Find the total number of items in two groups by counting all of them.
- Begin to relate addition to combining two groups of objects and subtraction to taking away.

Resources

- "Combining Two Groups" Notebook file
- "Two Sets" (p. 63)
- blank number cubes marked 1, 2, 3, 3, 4, 4 and counting toys for each pair of children

Whiteboard tools

- Pen tray
- Select tool
- Undo button

Getting Started

Go to page 2 of the "Combining Two Groups" Notebook file and use the Eraser from the Pen tray to rub over the first yellow shape to reveal the hidden objects. Encourage children to use the point-and-count technique and to say how many there are in total. Count again, together, with you pointing to (or highlighting) each item in turn. Repeat this for the next two sets of objects on the page. Repeat the activity on page 3.

Mini-Lesson

1. Go to page 4 of the Notebook file. Drag and drop three buttons into one empty set. Ask children to count as you do this and agree that there are three buttons. Now drag two buttons into the second empty set and repeat.

2. Ask: *How many are in this circle? And this one?* Explain that in order to find out how many there are altogether, children should count on from one of the circles. Ask them to count with you as you count again: *one, two, three; four and five. So there are five altogether.*

3. Press the Undo button until the page is reset and repeat for other examples. Use vocabulary such as *plus* and *makes, equals* and *totals*, as appropriate.

Independent Work

Invite children to work in pairs. Partners must take turns rolling the prepared number cubes twice (see Resources) and counting out the appropriate quantity of counting toys into each set circle on their copy of "Two Sets" (p. 63). They should then count how many there are in total, counting on from one set to the second. As children work, encourage them to say the addition number sentences for the quantities in front of them. For example, for four and two they would say: *One, two, three, four; five, six. So four plus two equals six.*

Limit younger or less-confident learners to number cubes marked 1, 1, 2, 2, 3, 3 and extend older or more-confident learners by using a traditional 1-to-6 number cube.

Wrap-Up

Return to page 4 of the Notebook file and repeat the activity from the Mini-Lesson. This time, ask children to say (from one to five) how many shapes to drag and drop into each circle. Invite confident learners to say aloud the counting and the addition number sentence. Display page 5 of the Notebook file and count the dots on the dominoes together. Encourage children to say the number sentences with you. Finally, go to page 6 and invite volunteers to come and add spots to the blank dominoes to make a number that you specify (up to five). Encourage the child, and then the rest of the class, to say the number sentence that goes with the arrangement.

Combining Three Groups

Learning objectives
- Count repeated groups of the same size.
- Begin to relate addition to combining two groups of objects and subtraction to taking away.

Resources
- "Combining Three Groups" Notebook file
- "Three Sets" (p. 64)
- 10 counting toys for each pair of children (12 for older or more-confident learners)

Whiteboard tools
- Pen tray
- Select tool
- Delete button
- Gallery

Getting Started

Go to page 2 of the "Combining Three Groups" Notebook file. Drag and drop objects into each of the set circles to make sets of three and four. Ask children to count each set by pointing. Say: *This set has three; let's count on to the other set to find the total.* Point to each shape as children count on and agree that three and four makes seven. Repeat this for other combinations.

If children are confident with this, ask them to count on for themselves, then to say the addition sentence. For example, for four and two they should say: *Four, five, six. So four and two makes six.* In subsequent sessions, repeat the activity using the three sets on page 3 of the Notebook file.

Mini-Lesson

1. Go to page 4 of the Notebook file to begin work on combining three groups. Ask children to count each set, then to say how many there are altogether by counting all of the objects.

2. Repeat the count for these three sets, this time asking children to count on from the first set. Ask: *Is the total the same?* Establish that we can count on to find totals for three sets. Where children are not yet confident with counting on, accept that they will probably, at this stage, count all of the objects.

3. Repeat this activity with further sets on pages 5 to 7.

4. Use pages 4 to 7 to develop the work with older or more-confident learners by asking them to use number sentences as they count and make the total. Encourage them to count the sets and then to say the number sentence that matches the arrangement. Use the Delete button (or select Delete from the drop-down menu) to remove the shapes at the bottom of the page to reveal the number sentences hidden underneath.

Independent Work

Arrange for children to work in pairs. Provide some counting toys and copies of "Three Sets" (p. 64). Invite partners to take turns taking a handful of counting toys and placing these on the sheet, dividing the toys among the three set circles. Their partner should count each set and find the total.

Suggest that younger or less-confident learners count all the objects at this stage. Provide older or more-confident learners with 12 counting toys.

Wrap-Up

Revisit pages 4 to 7 of the Notebook file from the Mini-Lesson. Ask children how they could find the total. Invite those who are able to count on from one set to demonstrate this. Repeat this for some other groups of three sets. Go to page 8 and add objects from the Gallery to create your own three sets. Invite individuals to come to the SMART Board and drag some shapes into each circle. Count them together.

Counting On

Learning objectives

- Know that a group of things changes in quantity when something is added or taken away.
- Begin to use the vocabulary involved in adding and subtracting.

Resources

- "Counting On" Notebook file
- "Two Sets" (p. 63)
- blank number cube labeled 1, 2, 2, 3, 3, 4
- 5 counting toys for each pair of children

Whiteboard tools

- Pen tray
- Select tool
- Undo button

Getting Started

Go to page 2 of the "Counting On" Notebook file. Drag two buttons into one set circle and ask children to count them. Drag three more buttons into the second set circle and repeat. Now find the total by counting all of the buttons. Encourage children to say the addition sentence: *Two plus three equals five.* Press the Undo button until the page is reset and repeat for other quantities up to five in each set circle.

Mini-Lesson

1. Go to page 3 of the Notebook file. Drag and drop some popsicles into each set circle (such as two into one and three into the other).

2. Ask children to count the first set, then the second, and to say how many there are in each.

3. Now count all: *One, two, three, four, five. So two plus three equals five.*

4. Repeat for other quantities.

5. Move on to page 4. Drag four popsicles into the left-hand circle and say: *I have put four popsicles in this circle.* Drag two popsicles into the right-hand circle and say: *I have put two popsicles in this circle. How many popsicles are there altogether?* Count on from four together to find out, saying: *Four, five, six. So four plus two equals six.*

6. Press the Undo button until the page is reset and repeat in the same way for other quantities, stating the quantity that is in the first circle, so that children count on from that number each time.

Independent Work

Pair up children and provide each pair with a prepared number cube (see Resources), a copy of "Two Sets" (p. 63), and five counting toys. Explain to children that they must take turns rolling the number cube and placing the matching number of toys into one of the set circles. The other child takes some of the toys and places those into the other set circle. Children then count on from the number on the number cube to find the total for the two sets.

Limit the number range for younger or less-confident learners by using number cubes marked 1, 1, 2, 2, 3, 3. For older or more-confident learners, provide standard 1-to-6 number cubes.

Wrap-Up

Go to page 5 of the Notebook file and press the number cube to roll it. Ask children to count the spots on the cube. Draw some more spots in the circle using a Pen from the Pen tray. Ask children to work out the total by counting on from the number of spots on the cube. Say the addition sentence together. Use the Eraser from the Pen tray to remove the spots from the circle and repeat the activity for other cube rolls. Add different numbers of spots to the circle, keeping the total between eight and ten.

Doubling

Learning objectives
- Find the total number of items in two groups by counting all of them.
- Count repeated groups of the same size.
- Begin to relate addition to combining two groups of objects.

Resources
- "Doubling" Notebook file
- blank number cube marked 1, 2, 3, 3, 4, 4 for each pair
- 1-to-6 number cube
- counting toys

Whiteboard tools
- Pen tray
- Select tool
- Undo button

Getting Started

Open the "Doubling" Notebook file and go to page 2. Say a number and ask children to draw it in the air, making it as large as they can. Write the number on the Notebook file. Invite children to repeat drawing the number in the air as you write on the SMART Board. Continue in this way, with other numbers between one and five.

Mini-Lesson

1. Reveal the set circles on page 3 of the Notebook file. Drag and drop two stars into each circle, so that both circles contain the same quantity.

2. Ask children to count how many stars there are in each circle. Agree that there are two in each circle.

3. Now count on from one circle to the other to find the total: *One, two, three, four. So two plus two is four.*

4. Repeat this for other quantities such as one plus one; three plus three.

5. Move on to page 4. Write a number 2 (for example) in the space provided above the left-hand circle, and drag this number of spots into the circle. Repeat for the right-hand circle. Count the spots together from two saying: *Two, and three, four. So two plus two is four.* Use a Pen from the Pen tray or a Highlighter pen to strike through the spots in the right-hand circle as you count.

6. Press the Undo button until the page is reset and repeat this for other doubles up to four. Encourage children to count on to find the total, using their fingers to help with the counting on at this stage if appropriate.

Independent Work

Arrange for children to work in pairs. Each pair will need a number cube marked 1, 2, 3, 3, 4, 4 (see Resources). Ask partners to take turns rolling the cube and counting on to find the total of the double. For example, if they roll a 3, they could count three more: *Three and four, five, six. So three plus three is six.*

Provide counting toys as well as the number cube for younger or less-confident learners to use. Suggest that they roll the cube, put out that quantity of toys, and count on from the cube's number using the toys as aids. Challenge older or more-confident learners to use a standard 1-to-6 number cube for finding doubles.

Wrap-Up

Challenge children to explain how they worked out the doubles. Invite volunteers to say a number sentence for a double, such as: *Four plus four equals eight.* Ask a child to roll the prepared number cube and say which number is shown. Encourage everyone to work out the double. Invite children to take turns saying the number sentence. For example, for double four they might say: *Four, and five, six, seven, eight. So four plus four equals eight.* Challenge the older or more-confident learners to find double five and double six and to explain to the others how they figured this out.

Totals

Learning objectives

- Find the total number of items in two groups by counting all of them.
- Begin to relate addition to combining two groups of objects.

Resources

- "Totals" Notebook file
- "Two Sets" (p. 63)
- empty margarine tub (or similar container)
- 10 counting toys for each pair of children

Whiteboard tools

- Pen tray
- Select tool
- Undo button

Getting Started

Open the "Totals" Notebook file and go to page 2. Drag and drop the objects into the set circles to make sets of four and two. Ask: *How can we find out how many there are altogether?* Start by counting all the objects together and then count on from one set. Press the Undo button until the page is reset and repeat the activity, changing the quantities to, for example, five and two.

Mini-Lesson

1. Move on to page 3 of the Notebook file. Use the Eraser from the Pen tray to reveal the number hidden in the left-hand circle (3). Say the number together.

2. Now drag and drop two popsicles into the right-hand circle. Say the revealed number again (3) and then ask children how many there are altogether.

3. Together, with you pointing to the popsicles in the right circle, count on from three. Then say: *Three plus two equals five.*

4. Repeat this for other quantities on pages 4 and 5, keeping the totals under ten (such as five and four; four and three).

Independent Work

Arrange for children to work in pairs. Provide each pair with a copy of "Two Sets" (p. 63), an empty margarine tub (or similar container), and ten counting toys. Invite children to take turns taking some toys and hiding them under the container, which they should then place on one of the circles on their sheet. Have them tell their partner how many toys they have hidden. Next, have them put some more toys onto the second circle. Their partner should calculate the total by counting on from the known, but hidden, set.

Limit the quantity of counting toys to up to six for younger or less-confident learners. Challenge older or more-confident learners to find several combinations for a larger total, such as nine. For example, seven (hidden) and two; five (hidden) and four; eight (hidden) and one.

Wrap-Up

Go to page 6 of the Notebook file. Invite a volunteer to come to the SMART Board and write a number on the left-hand set circle. Drag and drop some objects into the right-hand set circle, keeping the totals to no more than ten. Ask: *How shall we find the total?* Invite a child to demonstrate counting on from the numeral to find the total. Say the addition sentence together. Press the Undo button until the page is reset and repeat the activity, using other numbers and quantities.

Breaking Down Numbers

Learning objectives

- Share objects into equal groups and count how many in each group.
- Begin to use the vocabulary involved in adding and subtracting.

Resources

- "Breaking Down Numbers" Notebook file
- paper
- pens
- counting toys
- drawing materials

Whiteboard tools

- Pen tray
- Spotlight tool
- Select tool

Getting Started

Go to page 2 of the "Breaking Down Numbers" Notebook file and enable the Spotlight tool (so that the page is black, except for a small circle or rectangle). Move the spotlight and reveal one number at a time. Ask children to hold up that number of fingers. Repeat for other quantities within children's counting range. Repeat this activity over time, extending the range up to ten.

Mini-Lesson

1. Display page 3 of the Notebook file and explain that you will move some teddy bears into one side of the circle. Encourage children to count how many there are as you drag and drop them. Begin with all three teddy bears, and place them into one half of the circle. Ask: *How many teddy bears are there?*

2. Now move one of the teddy bears into the second part of the circle. Point to each part of the circle and ask: *How many are there here?* Then ask: *How many are there in total?* Agree that there are still three teddy bears. Say: *Two and one makes three.*

3. Repeat this with other combinations for three: one and two; two and one; three and zero; zero and three.

4. Use pages 4 to 6 to repeat for other combinations (totals of four, five, and six).

Independent Work

Arrange for children to work in pairs. Ask each pair to draw a circle with a line dividing it in half (like the one on the SMART Board) on a piece of paper. Provide some counting toys. Ask children to show you one way of separating five toys on the circle they have drawn. Can they think of another way? Leave the toys in the first arrangement and suggest that children draw another partitioned circle. Invite them to find another way to separate five toys. Continue to record the different ways by leaving the toys on the circles, drawing a new circle for each new way.

Limit younger or less-confident learners to finding different arrangements for three and four. Provide partitioned circles for them to use, rather than asking them to draw their own. Challenge older or more-confident learners to find different arrangements for six, once they have completed those for five.

Wrap-Up

Invite children to describe their arrangements for five. Demonstrate each one on the SMART Board using page 5 of the Notebook file. Ask children to count each set, then to count all to confirm that, for example, three and two makes five. Invite older or more-confident learners to describe their arrangements for six and demonstrate these using page 6.

Making Five

Learning objectives
- Select two groups of objects to make a given total of objects.
- Begin to relate addition to combining two groups of objects.

Resources
- "Making Five" Notebook file
- "Making Totals" (p. 65)
- counters for each child (two of each color available)

Whiteboard tools
- Eraser
- Pen tray
- Select tool
- Undo button

Getting Started
Open the "Making Five" Notebook file and go to page 2. Explain that you are going to clean the windows on the bus, one at a time (using the Eraser from the Pen tray), to find some hidden people. Tell children to wait until the people are all revealed and then ask them to point and count to find the quantity. Repeat for the other quantities that are concealed on pages 3 to 9 (including zero).

Mini-Lesson
1. Display the dogs under the empty sets on page 10 of the Notebook file. Count them together and agree that there are five.

2. Invite children to suggest how the dogs could be placed into the two circles. (0 + 5; 1 + 4; 2 + 3; 3 + 2; 4 + 1; 5 + 0)

3. Choose a suggestion and drag and drop the dogs into place. Say the addition sentence together for the relevant total of five.

4. Repeat this for the other totals of five. Check by counting on from one set to the other. Reset the page by repeatedly pressing the Undo button after each example.

Independent Work
Arrange for children to work in pairs. Give each pair a copy of "Making Totals" (p. 65) and some counters (two counters in each color available per child). Ask partners to take turns choosing two sets of animals from the sheet that they think will make a total of six. If their partner agrees, they may place matching counters onto each of the sets. (For example, if a child chooses a set of two elephants and a set of four camels to make a total of six, they should put one counter on the elephants and one counter of the same color on the camels.) As children work, encourage them to check their totals by counting on in ones from one set to the next.

Arrange for an adult to work with a group of younger or less-confident learners, with an 11" x 17" enlargement of the reproducible sheet. Suggest that children take turns finding two sets that make six. Ask them to check by counting as the adult points to the images. Challenge older or more-confident learners to find different totals for seven. Allow them to use counters to represent their pairs of sets.

Wrap-Up
Go back to page 10 of the Notebook file. Explain that you will drag and drop some dogs into one set circle. Ask children to decide how many more would be needed to make a total of, for example, four. They can count on, using their fingers to help if necessary, to find out what is missing. Drag the quantity of dogs that match children's answers into the other set circle. Check by counting on from the first set. Repeat this for other combinations for four.

Move on to page 11. Replace some red counters with yellow counters to show the different combinations that make a total of five. Discuss the pattern that is made as you change the color of one more counter in each row.

Taking Away

Learning objectives

- Show an interest in number problems.
- Know that a group of things changes in quantity when something is added or taken away.
- Begin to relate subtraction to taking away.

Resources

- "Taking Away" Notebook file
- "Counting Mat" (p. 56)
- counting toys

Whiteboard tools

- Pen tray
- Select tool
- Undo button

Getting Started

Open the "Taking Away" Notebook file and go to page 2. Use a Pen from the Pen tray, on a thick setting, to write any number between 1 and 6 on the page. Ask children to read the number, then to hold up that quantity of fingers. Repeat for other numbers from one to six. Extend this to up to ten over time.

Mini-Lesson

1. Move on to page 3 of the Notebook file. Drag and drop four dogs into the left-hand ring. Now say: *I am going to take away one of these. How many do you think will be left? How did you figure that out?*

2. Drag and drop one of the dogs from the left- to the right-hand set circle. Now ask: *How many did we start with? How many have we taken away? How many are left?*

3. Count together what is left and say: *Four take away one leaves three.*

4. Repeat this for other subtractions from four, such as 4 – 2; 4 – 3; 4 – 4.

Independent Work

Invite children to work in pairs. They will need a copy of the "Counting Mat" (p. 56) and five counting toys. Ask partners to take turns placing all five toys on the counting mat. Have one partner say how many to take away, and then both predict how many are left, before counting. Encourage them to say the appropriate subtraction sentence after each turn. Help children to repeat this for different subtractions from five: 5 – 0; 5 – 1; 5 – 2; 5 – 3; 5 – 4; 5 – 5.

Show children the five rows of five colored counters on page 4 of the Notebook file. Demonstrate taking away different numbers from five by moving counters to the side of the page. Follow a pattern by taking away one, then two, three, four, and five. What pattern do children notice?

Reinforce subtraction from two, three, and four with younger or less-confident learners. Challenge older or more-confident learners to try this for subtraction from six.

Wrap-Up

Discuss what happens when subtracting zero. Agree that nothing changes because nothing has been taken away. Model this on page 3 of the Notebook file by dragging five dogs into one set circle. Next, discuss what happens when subtracting all. Agree that all are taken away, so nothing (or zero) is left. Reset page 3 by repeatedly pressing the Undo button and demonstrate again with the dogs. Having shown children what happens when subtracting all, reset the page again and demonstrate further examples. Each time, ask children to say what will be left before the images are taken away.

Counting Back

Learning objectives

- Know that a group of things changes in quantity when something is added or taken away.
- Begin to use the vocabulary involved in adding and subtracting.

Resources

- "Counting Back" Notebook file
- "Two Sets" (p. 63)
- 10 counting toys for each pair of children

Whiteboard tools

- Pen tray
- Select tool
- Undo button
- Gallery

Getting Started

Go to page 2 of the "Counting Back" Notebook file. Drag and drop four objects into the left-hand circle. Say: *I am going to take away one of these. How many do you think will be left? How did you figure that out?* Drag one of the images from the left- to the right-hand circle. Now ask: *How many did we start with? How many have we taken away? So how many are left?* Count together what is left and say: *Four take away one leaves three.* Press the Undo button until the page is reset and repeat, keeping the total to no more than ten objects.

Mini-Lesson

1. Reset the page using the Undo button and move five images into the left-hand circle. Encourage children to count how many there are by pointing. Say: *I am going to take away two of the objects.* Drag two images into the other circle.

2. Explain that another way to find out what is left after taking away is to count back from the larger number. Pointing to the images in the right-hand circle, count back two from five: *Four, three: so there are three left. Five take away two leaves three.* Check by counting what is in the left-hand circle.

3. Repeat this for other starting quantities and amounts to take away.

Independent Work

Ask children to work in pairs. Each pair will need ten counting toys and a copy of "Two Sets (p. 63). Invite one child from each pair to take some counting toys (for example, six) and place them in one of the circles. Children should count the toys and agree how many there are. The second child should move some of the toys (for example, three) to the second circle. They count back from the total (six) for the number in the second circle (three) to find out how many are left. Encourage children to say the subtraction sentence. For example: *Six take away three leaves three.* Invite children to leave their final subtraction on the activity sheet in front of them so that these can be used in the Wrap-Up.

Limit younger or less-confident learners to no more than six counting toys. Challenge older or more-confident learners to take away larger quantities from eight, nine, or ten.

Wrap-Up

Invite a child to say how many counting toys they began with and how many they subtracted. Model this on the SMART Board, using page 3 of the Notebook file and images from the Gallery. Invite another child to demonstrate the counting-back procedure and to say the subtraction sentence. Repeat for other children's subtraction sentences.

How Many Are Left?

Learning objectives

- Know that a group of things changes in quantity when something is added or taken away.
- Begin to use the vocabulary involved in adding and subtracting.

Resources

- "How Many Are Left?" Notebook file
- "Two Sets" (p. 63)
- 10 counting toys and an empty margarine tub (or similar container) for each pair of children

Whiteboard tools

- Pen tray
- Select tool
- Undo button

Getting Started

Open the "How Many Are Left?" Notebook file and go to page 2. Drag and drop six shapes into the left-hand circle and ask: *How many shapes are there?* Now drag two of these into the right-hand circle. Say: *How many shapes have I taken away? How can we find out what is left?* Agree that children can find out by counting the shape. Say together: *Six take away two leaves four.* Repeat for other quantities between three and ten.

Mini-Lesson

1. Go to page 3 of the Notebook file where the left-hand set circle contains a hidden number. Reveal the hidden number (3) using the Eraser from the Pen tray. Now drag and drop one object into the right-hand circle.

2. Ask: *How many were there in this?* (Point to the left-hand circle.) *How many have we taken away?* (Point to the right-hand circle.)

3. Explain that in order to find out how many are left, children can count up from what has been taken away. Suggest that they use their fingers to help them keep track of the count. So, for this example, say: *Two, three. So two are left. Three take away one leaves two.*

4. Repeat this, using the other hidden numbers on pages 4 and 5 as starting points. (For example, for page 4 drag three objects into the right-hand circle and count up: *Four, five. So five take away three leaves two.*)

5. Extend the activity by using the empty set circles on page 6. Write a chosen number in the left-hand circle and place some objects (a smaller amount) in the right-hand circle. Encourage children to figure out how many are left if you take the second number away from the first.

Independent Work

Have children work in pairs. Each pair will need an empty margarine tub (or similar container), up to ten counting toys, and a copy of "Two Sets" (p. 63). Partners take turns taking some of the counting toys and counting how many they have, then telling their partner the total. They should then hide some of the toys under the container on one of the circles and place the rest on the other circle. Have the other child calculate what is hidden by counting up from what they can see to the known total.

Limit younger or less-confident learners to up to six counting toys. Challenge older or more-confident learners by giving them twelve counting toys.

Wrap-Up

Display page 7 of the Notebook file and tell children that this time you will simply write the numbers into the set circles. Write 6 in the left-hand circle and 3 in the right-hand one. Say: *There were six cupcakes on the plate. Three cupcakes were eaten. How many were left?* Invite children to find the answer by counting up. If necessary, drag and drop the cupcakes into the circles to check answers or to support younger or less-confident learners. Repeat for other totals within ten, giving counting toys to children who need them.

How Many More?

Learning objectives
- Show an interest in number problems.
- Use language such as *more* or *less* to compare two numbers.

Resources
- "How Many More?" (p. 66)

Whiteboard tools
- Pen tray
- Select tool
- Undo button
- Shapes tool

Before You Start
Prepare a Notebook file by using the Shapes tool to add two large circles side-by-side on the page. Then select Lock in Place from the drop-down menu to keep them in place on the page.

Getting Started
Display your prepared Notebook file (see Before You Start). Use a Pen from the Pen tray to write a total in the left-hand circle and a smaller number in the right-hand one. Write, for example, the numbers 6 and 2 and say: *There are six rabbits in the rabbit hole. Two of them go out into the garden. How many rabbits are left in the rabbit hole?* Encourage children to work out the answer by counting up. Suggest that they keep track on their fingers as they count, if necessary.

Mini-Lesson
1. Explain to children that today they will be learning about counting up to find the answers to some problems.

2. Press the Undo button to reset the Notebook page and write 3 in the left-hand circle and 7 in the right-hand circle. Say: *We have three laces. There are seven children who want to make a necklace with the beads. How many more laces do we need?*

3. Discuss how to solve this by counting up from three to seven. Children may find it useful, at this stage, to keep track of how many they count with their fingers. Say together: *Four, five, six, seven. We counted four more. So we need four more laces.*

4. Reset the page and repeat this for other examples of word problems where children have to count up to find the answer.

Independent Work
Organize children to work in groups of four to six with an adult. Provide the adult with a copy of "How Many More?" (p. 66). The adult should read each problem to the children. Children who are still unsure about keeping a mental tally when counting up should be encouraged to use their fingers at this stage to keep track of how many.

Simplify the word problems with lower numbers for younger or less-confident learners, and challenge older or more-confident learners by increasing the higher number up to twelve.

Wrap-Up
Explain that you will give some more word problems. Again, write the numbers into the circles on the SMART Board. Say the following problems aloud and invite children to tell you the answer:

- *There are four cups. Eight children want a drink. How many more cups do we need?*

- *Seven elephants would like a bun each. There are only three buns. How many more buns are needed?*

Ask more questions like these.

Pick the Larger Number

Getting Started

Display page 2 of the "Pick the Larger Number" Notebook file. Point to each pair of numbers in order, asking: *Which is the larger number?* Ask volunteers to press on the number agreed upon. They will hear a cheer if they are correct.

Mini-Lesson

1. Go to page 3 of the Notebook file. Invite children to say the numbers from 1 to 10, in order, and ask for volunteers to write these into the track.

2. Now write the addition sentence 5 + 2. Point to the number 5 on the track and say: *To find five plus two, start at five and count on two. So, five, six, seven. 5 + 2 = 7.* Point to the numbers on the track as you count on.

3. Repeat this for other examples, keeping the total to about seven or eight.

4. Write 3 + 4 on the board and explain that it is easier to begin with the larger number. Ask: *Which is larger, three or four?* Count on along the track, starting at four and counting on three.

5. Repeat this for other examples.

6. Hide the number track using the Screen Shade and ask children to try the next example mentally. Say: *two plus five.* Agree that it will be easier to start at five, the larger number. Say together: *five and six, seven. So 2 + 5 = 7.*

7. Use the number cube to generate other examples, with children working mentally.

Independent Work

Give out copies of "Larger Number First" (p. 67). Provide each pair of children with a 1-to-6 number cube and a set of 1-to-4 numeral cards. Explain the activity: Children take turns tossing the number cube and choosing one of the cards at random. Then they make an addition sentence from the two numbers, putting the larger number first before finding the total.

Decide whether or not to limit the number range for less-confident learners by providing two sets of numeral cards 1 to 4. Extend the range for more-confident learners by providing two 1-to-6 number cubes for each pair to use. Choose some of the completed tables to scan into the computer for the Wrap-Up.

Wrap-Up

Ask children to review scanned examples on the SMART Board. Invite individual children to say aloud how to add, starting from the larger number. Repeat, using other examples from children's work. Try another couple of examples with the on-screen number cube. Use page 4 of the Notebook file to assess children's understanding of what they have learned during the lesson.

Learning objective
- Count on or back in ones.

Resources
- "Pick the Larger Number" Notebook file
- "Larger Number First" (p. 67)
- pencils
- 1-to-6 number cube and 1-to-4 numeral cards, for each pair of children

Whiteboard tools
- Pen tray
- Select tool
- Screen Shade

Solving Problems

Learning objectives
- Solve problems involving adding.
- Describe ways of solving puzzles and problems, explaining choices and decisions orally or using pictures.

Resources
- "Writing Addition Sentences" (p. 68)
- 8 counters each for less-confident learners

Whiteboard tools
- Pen tray
- Select tool
- Gallery (Use the goldfish image in the Gallery for work in the Wrap-Up activity.)

Getting Started

Explain that you are going to write two numbers on the SMART Board, and you would like children to add them together. Remind them to put the larger number first and count on in ones: 2 + 6; 5 + 3; 1 + 7; 4 + 5. Invite a volunteer to say the total each time and to explain how he or she figured out the answer.

Mini-Lesson

1. Explain that today's lesson is about solving problems. Ask: *How many different ways can we find for making the number ten?* Invite suggestions and write these on the SMART Board.

2. Make a list of different ways of making ten. For example, 6 + 4; 5 + 5; 2 + 8. More-confident learners may suggest some subtraction sentences, too.

3. Ask children to explain how they worked out their responses. Discuss mental methods, including putting the larger number first and counting on in ones. Change numbers around to put the larger number first.

4. Repeat for another problem, such as: *I have some number cards for the numbers 1 to 6. How many ways can I make 7 using two cards each time?* Invite children to suggest ways this can be done.

Independent Work

Give out copies of "Writing Addition Sentences" (p. 68). Read the problem through and ask for suggestions for solving it. Have children work in pairs to complete the reproducible.

Decide whether to provide counters for less-confident learners to arrange into the circles on the sheet. They can record their arrangements as addition sentences. Challenge more-confident learners, when they have completed the main task, to arrange eight fish into three circles. They can draw and write their responses on the back of the sheet.

Wrap-Up

Invite children from each ability group to suggest solutions. Draw each solution and its number sentence on the SMART Board. Continue until all possible solutions have been found. These are: 0 + 8; 1 + 7; 2 + 6; 3 + 5; 4 + 4; 5 + 3; 6 + 2; 7 + 1; 8 + 0. Now invite the more-confident learners to explain the challenge that they were set in the Independent Work. Ask all children to think about how they could solve this. Draw and write solutions on the SMART Board. For example, 2 + 3 + 3; 5 + 2 + 1; and so on.

Tens and Ones

Getting Started

Provide children with the ten single-digit cards (0 to 9) in the set made from "Digit Cards" (p. 69). Go to page 2 of the "Tens and Ones" Notebook file. Read the story with children. Ask them to look out for sentences with a number word. At the end of those sentences, they must hold up the correct digit card when you say *Show me*.

Invite a child to come to the SMART Board and use the Eraser from the Pen tray to reveal the numeral at the end of the sentence to see if he or she was right. Read the question at the end of the story. Count up the pictures of the presents together. Use the Eraser to check the answer. Invite children to hold up the correct digit card for this number.

Mini-Lesson

1. Introduce the cards for 10, 20, and 30. Discuss what the digits on each card represent (for example, 10 means "one ten and no ones"). Show children how to make a "teen" or "twenty something" by placing one of the 0 to 9 cards over the zero placeholder on the 10 or 20 cards.

2. Go to page 3 of the Notebook file. Read each sentence, looking for number words. This time, ask children to say as well as show you the numbers. Ask them to say how many tens and how many ones are needed to make the numbers. Invite a child to use the Eraser to reveal the answer.

3. Count the friends to find out how many guests have been invited altogether.

4. Repeat the activity on page 4.

Independent Work

Ask children to work in groups of four. They will need a set of "Digit Cards" (p. 69), paper, and pencils for recording. Children should write a sentence that includes a teen number. Display page 5 of the Notebook file, which provides the numbers and number words to 20. Check that children can spot the number word that they need.

Decide whether to limit the number range for less-confident learners to numbers up to ten. Challenge more-confident learners to extend the range to 30. If necessary, provide a card with the number words written on it. Scan some of the sentences for the Wrap-Up.

Wrap-Up

Begin by reviewing some of children's sentences from the Independent Work. Invite everyone to read the number words and to show the numbers using the digit cards. Go to page 6 of the Notebook file to finish the story of Mark's party. Ask children to show each number word using their digit cards. Once they have done this, use the Eraser to reveal the answers on the screen.

Learning objectives
- Read and write numerals from 0 to 20, then beyond.
- Use knowledge of place value.

Resources
- "Tens and Ones" Notebook file
- "Digit Cards" (p. 69), copied onto cardstock and cut apart
- writing materials

Whiteboard tools
- Eraser
- Pen tray
- Select tool

Grouping for Easy Addition

Learning objectives

- Relate addition to counting on.
- Use practical and informal written methods to support the addition of a one-digit number to a one-digit or two-digit number.
- Use the vocabulary related to addition and symbols to describe and record addition number sentences.

Resources

- "Grouping for Easy Addition" Notebook file
- "Splitting Numbers" (p. 70)
- number lines or tracks for less-confident learners

Whiteboard tools

- Pen tray
- Select tool
- Gallery

Getting Started

Open page 2 of the "Grouping for Easy Addition" Notebook file. Ask children to suggest addition sentences that will give 6 as the total—for example, 4 + 2. Write the sentences on the SMART Board. Discuss how children worked out their answers. Repeat the activity for sums of 7, 8, and 9.

Mini-Lesson

1. Go to page 3 of the Notebook file. Ask: *What should I add to five to make six?* Write 5 + 1 underneath the strawberries, and demonstrate this number sentence using the strawberry images (you can add another strawberry by dragging one from any of the existing strawberries).

2. Go to page 4 and repeat this process for seven strawberries: 5 + 2.

3. Move to page 5. Write 6 + 7 = 5 + 1 + 5 + 2. Ask: *How can I figure out the answer?* Move the white boxes together to encourage children to combine the 5s in the top halves to make 10, and then add the 1 and 2 in the lower halves. Write 5 + 5 = 10, 1 + 2 = 3. 10 + 3 = 13. Demonstrate, and allow children to try this using the strawberries.

4. Write the total of 13. Say together: *6 + 7 is the same as 5 + 1 + 5 + 2, which is 10 + 3. The total is 13.*

5. Repeat for pages 6 and 7 of the Notebook file. Add objects from the Gallery or drag and drop the object at the top of each page.

Independent Work

Provide each pair of children with a copy of "Splitting Numbers" (p. 70). Working in pairs, have children take turns choosing two numbers from the grid, writing a number sentence, and figuring out the answer. Remind them to split each number into "five and a bit."

Decide whether to limit less-confident learners to adding 1, 2, 3, 4 to 6, 7, 8, 9. Work together as a group to practice counting on in ones: 6 + 4. 6 is 5 + 1. So 5 + 1 + 4 is 5 + 5. If children do not know the answer, they should count on in ones to find it. Alternatively, they can use a number line to help them. Challenge more-confident learners to total three numbers (such as 6 + 6 + 7) using the "five and a bit" method.

Wrap-Up

Review some of the number sentences children have written. Write these on page 8 of the Notebook file, without the answers. Challenge the other children to say how to figure out the answers. Use counters from the Gallery if necessary. Divide the class into two teams. Explain that each team can choose two numbers from five to nine for the other team to add. Give a point to each team for a correct answer.

Making Ten

Learning objectives
- Derive and recall all pairs of numbers with a total of 10.
- Use practical and informal written methods to support the addition of a one-digit number to a one-digit or two-digit number.

Resources
- "Making Ten" Notebook file
- "Make a Ten" (p. 71)

Whiteboard tools
- Pen tray
- Select tool

Getting Started

Say some addition sentences and ask children to say the answers. Use facts that they are beginning to know, such as addition facts for 10 (6 + 4, 2 + 8, and so on); addition doubles up to 5 + 5; all addition facts up to 5 + 5 (4 + 3, 2 + 4, and so on). Use the ten-space track on page 2 of the "Making Ten" Notebook file if children are uncertain. Discuss how the answer could be found by counting on in ones from the larger number.

Mini-Lesson

1. Go to page 3 of the Notebook file. Write the numbers 1 to 20 into the track. Ask: *How shall we figure out 6 + 7?* Agree that you could count on in ones from the larger number (7 + 6).

2. Count on in ones from seven, and agree that the answer is 13.

3. Explain that there is another way to do this. Write 6 + 7 = __. Then say: *We can make a 10 like this: 7 is the same as 4 plus 3 . . .* (write 6 + 4 + 3) *6 + 4 = 10, and 3 more is 13.*

4. Repeat this for other examples that cross the 10 boundary (for example, 5 + 8 and 6 + 9). Each time, encourage children to use the new method first, and write up the expanded number sentence. Check by counting along the number track, beginning with the larger number.

Independent Work

Give out copies of "Make a Ten" (p. 71). Have children work in pairs to make eight number sentences using the numbers on the sheet and to solve them using the new method.

Decide whether or not to work with the less-confident learners as a group. Encourage them to use mental strategies, then to check their answers, counting on in ones from the larger number, either mentally or using a number track. Challenge more-confident learners to try some examples that cross the 20 boundary, such as 19 + 3 or 17 + 6.

Wrap-Up

Go to page 4 of the Notebook file. Invite a volunteer to read out a number sentence, without giving the expanded number sentence or the answer. Write it up and ask the other children to decide how to figure out the problem. Write out the relevant expanded number sentence. For example, 6 + 8 = 6 + 4 + 4 = 10 + 4 = 14. Repeat for other examples. Over time, extend this to crossing the 20 boundary.

Coins

Learning objectives

- Show an interest in number problems.
- Begin to use the vocabulary involved in adding and subtracting.

Resources

- "Coins" Notebook file
- "Counting Coins" (p. 72)
- sets of coins for each group of children (pennies, nickels, dimes, and quarters)
- plastic cups to put the coins in
- 1-to-6 number cubes

Whiteboard tools

- Pen tray
- Select tool
- Delete button
- Undo button

Getting Started

Divide the class into small groups and provide each group with a set of mixed coins. Open the "Coins" Notebook file and go to page 2. Point to one of the coins on the page and ask children to find that coin in their cup. Ask: *What is this coin called? What color is it? What pictures can you see on it?* Press on the coin on the screen and use the Delete button (or select the Delete option from the drop-down menu) to reveal what is on the reverse. Repeat for the other coins on the Notebook page.

Mini-Lesson

1. Go to page 3 of the Notebook file. Point to the cherries and ask how much they are. Invite a volunteer to come to the SMART Board and drag the correct amount into the purse below the cherries. If the child suggests two nickels (5¢ coins), accept this, but also point out that the dime (10¢ coin) is worth the same as two nickels.

2. Repeat the activity for the other items on the page.

3. Point to the 25¢ apple. Ask: *Can you find some different ways to pay for this?* Encourage children to show you the correct change by placing the coins in front of them (five nickels; two dimes and one nickel; one dime and three nickels; one quarter; etc.).

4. Move on to page 4 and invite volunteers to come and show the different ways to pay for the 25¢ apple by dragging and dropping coins into the four purses.

Independent Work

Have children work in pairs. Each pair will need a cup of 20 pennies, a 1-to-6 number cube, and a copy of "Counting Coins" (p. 72). Invite partners to take turns rolling the number cube. Tell them to take the number they rolled in pennies and place them on the stars. The first person to collect 10¢ wins the game.

Arrange for an adult to work with younger or less-confident learners to check that they can count how many coins they have for each throw of the number cube and for their total each time. Challenge older or more-confident learners to say how many more coins they need each time to reach their goal.

Wrap-Up

Go to page 5 of the Notebook file, point to the cereal bar, and read the price label. Ask children to suggest ways that they could pay for the cereal bar. Invite individuals to come to the SMART Board and drag coins that add up to the value of 50¢ into the purses. How many ways can they find? Press the Undo button until the page is reset. Ask if children can think of more than five ways to pay. Suggest that children put out real coins in front of themselves for each new combination.

What Comes Between?

Learning objectives
- Use some number language such as *more* and *a lot.*
- Use language such as *more* or *less* to compare two numbers.

Resources
- "What Comes Between?" Notebook file
- "What Fits?" (p. 73)
- two colors of counters and crayons for each pair of children

Whiteboard tools
- Eraser
- Pen tray
- Select tool

Getting Started

Display the two sets on page 2 of the "What Comes Between?" Notebook file. Compare the quantities. Ask children to count both sets by pointing and saying how many are in each. Ask: *Which set has more? Which set has fewer?* Repeat the activity using page 3.

Mini-Lesson

1. Go to page 4 of the Notebook file and invite a child to come and move some objects (up to six) into one of the set circles. Invite another child to come up and move some objects into the other set circle. Ask: *Which set has more/fewer?*

2. Continue in this way with the set circles and objects on pages 5 and 6. (Page 6 contains 17 objects, so the first child can move up to eight objects into the first set.)

3. Next, reveal the blank number track on page 7. Explain that you will write the numbers from 1 to 10 on the track and that you would like children to write each number in the air, using their whole arm, as you do this.

4. Now ask children to read the numbers as you point to them in number order.

5. Next, use the Eraser from the Pen tray to erase the numbers. Write most of them in again but leave one or two blank. Ask, for example: *Which number fits between 3 and 5?* (Write in 4.) *Which number fits between 7 and 9?* (Write in 8.)

6. Repeat this game, erasing more of the numbers this time. Invite children to say what each missing number is as you point to the spaces.

Independent Work

Provide each pair with colored crayons, counters, and a copy of "What Fits?" (p. 73). Have one partner choose an empty square on the number track. The other partner must say the missing number. If they both agree, one partner should write in the number. Have partners continue taking turns until the track is complete. Display the completed number track on page 8 of the Notebook file to provide support.

Ask an adult to work with younger or less-confident learners. Provide them with an 11" x 17" enlargement of the sheet, and suggest that children take turns choosing a square on the track and say, then write, the number. Challenge older or more-confident learners to play the game quickly, so that they recall the numbers, and their positions, as quickly as possible.

Wrap-Up

Go back to page 7 of the Notebook file and the blank number track. Invite individuals to come to the SMART Board and write numbers in the correct places. Complete the track in this way. Now erase the numbers and ask children to work mentally. Say: *What number comes between 1 and 3 . . . 5 and 7 . . .* and so on. Show children the jumbled-up track on page 9. Invite them to drag and drop the numbers into the correct positions on the blank number track above.

Ordering Sets

Learning objectives
- Count up to three or four objects by saying one number name for each item.
- Say and use number names in order in familiar contexts.

Resources
- "Ordering Sets" Notebook file
- 12 disposable cups or margarine tubs and 4 sets of counting toys, such as cubes, beads, shape tiles, and construction bricks, for each pair of children

Whiteboard tools
- Pen tray
- Screen Shade
- Highlighter pen
- Select tool

Getting Started

Open the "Ordering Sets" Notebook file and go to page 2. Ask children to count each set by pointing. Then ask: *Which set has more stars? How many more? Which set has fewer stars? How many fewer?* When children have agreed on the correct answer, move the Screen Shade to reveal the bottom pair of sets and repeat. Continue with the pairs of sets on pages 3 and 4.

Mini-Lesson

1. Go to page 5 of the Notebook file. Drag and drop the three sets of images (a set of five, a set of three, and a set of two) from the box onto the screen, so that they are not in quantity order.

2. Ask children to count each set and to agree how many stars are in each one. Ask: *Which set has fewest?* Invite a child to come and drag and drop that set to the left side of the page.

3. Ask: *Which set has most?* Invite another child to drag that set to the right side of the page. Ask: *Where does the set with three stars belong?* Agree that it goes between the other two sets. Invite a third child to move this set into the middle.

4. Discuss how the sets are now in number order.

5. Repeat for the other sets of images on pages 6 to 8.

Independent Work

Ask children to work in pairs. They will need 12 disposable cups and four different sets of counting toys. Ask them to make three sets of different numbers of cubes (for example) by putting each set into a cup. Explain that they must order the sets, starting with the smallest number.

Ensure that an adult works with younger or less-confident learners, carrying out the task as a group. Encourage children to use the vocabulary of ordering as they work. Encourage children to continue working with their partners to sort the other three sets of sorting toys. Challenge older or more-confident learners to make four or five sets each time and to order these.

Wrap-Up

Invite some children of different ability levels to count out each of their sets and to explain how they have ordered them. Finish by going to pages 9 and 10 of the Notebook file. Drag and drop up to six sets out of the boxes and invite children to count by pointing, and then order these from least to most.

Ordering Numbers

Learning objectives
- Use some number names accurately in play.
- Know that numbers identify how many objects are in a set.
- Say and use number names in order in familiar contexts.

Resources
- "Ordering Numbers" Notebook file
- counting toys

Whiteboard tools
- Pen tray
- Undo button
- Select tool

Getting Started

Go to page 2 of the "Ordering Numbers" Notebook file and look at the empty number train together. Drag the numbers 1, 4, 7, and 10 into their correct places. Ask children to decide which numbers fit in the spaces. Drag and drop the numbers as children say them. Repeat until the train is complete. Press on the funnel when you've finished to hear the sound of a train tooting. Press the Undo button until the page is reset and start again with a different combination of numbers.

Mini-Lesson

1. Display the set of images on page 3 of the Notebook file. Ask children to count the number of triangles in each set by pointing. Ask: *How many are in each set?*

2. Next, ask: *Which is the smallest set?* Drag and drop this onto the empty circle on the left side of the page. Ask: *Which is the largest?* Drag and drop this onto the empty circle on the right. Can children tell you where the last set goes? Agree that it belongs in the middle and that the sets are now in number order.

3. Repeat for the sets on pages 4 to 6.

4. Go to page 7. Look at the empty circle in the middle and the sets at either side. Discuss what number of stars should go in the middle set. Invite a volunteer to come to the SMART Board and drag and drop a suitable number of stars into place.

5. Repeat the activity on pages 8 and 9. (On page 9, there is more than one possible correct answer.)

Independent Work

Go to page 10 of the Notebook file and look at the shirts on the washing line. Ask: *What numbers could go in the empty shirts?* Invite a child to come and select and drag the correct number to fill the empty shirt. Invite more children to do the same using pages 11 and 12.

Have children work in groups of four and provide each group with some counting toys. Ask each child to make a set of between one and ten toys. Each set in their group must have a different quantity of toys, so they will need to negotiate this with one another. Encourage them to order their sets of toys, putting the smallest quantity first. Repeat the activity three more times. As children work, invite each group to explain how they know that their sets are in number order.

Suggest that younger or less-confident learners order quantities of up to six objects. Challenge older or more-confident learners to order six sets.

Wrap-Up

Ask one group to choose one of their ordered sets and to whisper the quantities to you. Write these numbers up, out of order, in the boxes on page 13 of the Notebook file. Invite the other children to verbally order the numbers, from least to most. When children agree, allow one child to drag the numbers into the correct order. Go to page 14 of the Notebook file. Invite individuals to come to the SMART Board, select a number, and drop it in the right place on the washing line.

Number Order

Learning objectives

- Read and write numerals from 0 to 20, then beyond.
- Use knowledge of place value to position these numbers on a number track.

Resources

- "Number Order" Notebook file
- "Number Tracks" (p. 74)

Whiteboard tools

- Eraser
- Pen tray
- Select tool

Getting Started

Display page 2 of the "Number Order" Notebook file. Reveal the numbers slowly by pulling the tab on the left-hand side of the page. Ask children to say each number as it appears. Point to one of the numerals and ask children to draw it in the air. Watch to check that they do this correctly and invite a child who is confident at this to write up the numeral on the Notebook page.

Mini-Lesson

1. Go to page 3 of the Notebook file. Point out the start number (1) in the first box. Explain to children that you would like them to say what number should come next, and next, and so on. Write in the numbers to 10 in sequence, as children say them.

2. Use the Eraser from the Pen tray to remove the numbers from the track. Write the number 5 in its correct position on the track. Ask: *What number comes after/before 5?* Invite volunteers to come to the SMART Board to write in the missing numbers. Continue until all the numbers to 10 are in place.

3. Erase the numbers in the track and go to page 4. Point out the 7 at the beginning of the track and the 12 in the final space. Invite children to suggest what numbers are missing and where these fit. Write them in. Read together the numbers on the line and agree that these are in number order, even though this track doesn't begin with 1 or 0.

4. Repeat the activity on page 5 for other number ranges, increasing the range to up to 20.

Independent Work

Give out copies of "Number Tracks" (p. 74) for children to complete. As they work, ask questions such as: *How do you know that this number fits there? What number is one more/less than ___? Where would it fit on this number line?*

Work with the less-confident learners as a group. They can recite the counting numbers in order, from the start number until they reach the missing number. Challenge more-confident learners to write numbers in order, from 15 to about 30, on the back of their sheet.

Wrap-Up

Show the ten-space number track on page 6 of the Notebook file, and write in the number: 4 in the second space, 7 in the fifth space, and 10 in the eighth space. Ask: *How can we work out what numbers are missing?* Listen to children's suggestions, writing in the one before and one after for each number. Then invite them to say what the last missing number is. (12) Repeat this for a different number range, such as 7 to 16. Erase the numbers in the track. Write 15 in the fifth space. Ask: *How could we find out what the first number will be? What about the last number?* Ask for volunteers to write in the numbers.

Sorting

Learning objectives
- Sort objects, making choices and justifying decisions.
- Use developing mathematical ideas and methods to solve practical problems.

Resources
- "Sorting" Notebook file
- "Counting Mat" (p. 56)
- sorting toys

Whiteboard tools
- Pen tray
- Select tool
- Undo button

Getting Started

Drag and drop some houses onto the counting mat on page 2 of the "Sorting" Notebook file. Ask children to count how many houses there are. Now say: *If I add one more, how many houses will there be then?* Invite children to tell you, then drag and drop one more house onto the counting mat. Ask children to check by counting on. Use the Undo button to revert the screen to the beginning and repeat for different totals (keep the totals to no more than about eight).

Mini-Lesson

1. Move on to page 3 of the Notebook file. Look at the different types and colors of houses. Encourage children to describe each of the houses by its color, size, and shape.

2. Say: *We need to sort the houses. All the yellow houses need to go into the circle.* Following children's instructions, drag and drop the houses that they suggest into the set circle.

3. Ask: *Have we found all the yellow houses? Are all the yellow houses the same as one another? How are they different? What about the houses that are outside the circle? Are these yellow? Do they belong in the circle? Why not?*

4. Repeat this using another sorting criterion, such as all the apartment buildings or all the bungalows. Invite volunteers to come and drag the objects into the set circle.

Independent Work

Arrange for children to work in pairs. Provide each pair with a "Counting Mat" (p. 56) and some toys to sort. Ask children to find different ways to sort their toys.

Limit the range of toys for younger or less-confident learners so that they have fewer properties to sort. Challenge older or more-confident learners to sort their toys by two properties, such as: *Is a house and is yellow.*

Ask children to keep their favorite way of sorting the toys for the Wrap-Up session.

Wrap-Up

Give children a few minutes to look at one another's favorite sorting methods. Ask them to choose one of the other children's methods and to be ready to explain how the toys have been sorted. Invite children to explain how other children have sorted their toys. Encourage them to express this as a sentence (for example, *Kendra sorted all the toys that are animals*). Show the selection of objects and the set circle on page 4 of the Notebook file. Choose a sorting criterion, but do not tell children what it is. Drag and drop some of the objects into the set circle and ask: *How have I sorted these?* Repeat for other criteria, or invite individuals to choose a criterion. Each time, encourage children to explain in one sentence the criteria for sorting.

Making Patterns

- Show an interest in shape and space by making arrangements with objects.
- Talk about, recognize, and recreate simple patterns.
- Use developing mathematical ideas and methods to solve practical problems.

Resources
- "Making Patterns" Notebook file
- "Follow the Patterns" (p. 75)
- laces and shape beads (cubes, cuboids, cylinders, spheres) for each child

Whiteboard tools
- Pen tray
- Select tool
- Fill Color tool
- Undo button

Getting Started
Go to page 2 of the "Making Patterns" Notebook file and ask questions such as: *What color is the second bead? Which bead is between the second and fourth? What color would the next bead in the pattern be?* Invite volunteers to come and drag the next bead into the sequence. Continue with two or three more beads and volunteers.

Mini-Lesson
1. Move on to page 3 of the Notebook file. Invite children to describe the pattern. Ask: *What would come next in the pattern? How do you know that? What is the third animal? What comes between the third and fifth animals?*

2. Now go to page 4 and encourage children to describe the pattern. Ask them to shut their eyes. Drag and drop a shape tile over the fourth element of the sequence. Invite children to open their eyes and tell you what has been covered up. Repeat, covering other elements.

3. Display the 3D shapes on page 5. Ask children to describe the 3D shape pattern and then drag and drop some more shapes to continue the sequence. Repeat the activity from page 4 by using the blocks to cover different elements of the sequence.

Independent Work
Show children the shapes on page 6 of the Notebook file. Invite individuals to come to the SMART Board and use the Fill Color tool to change the color of some of the shapes to create a color pattern. Next, provide each child with laces and beads, together with a copy of "Follow the Patterns" (p. 75). Challenge children to follow the patterns shown on the reproducible page as they thread their laces. If the different-shaped beads are not available, ask children to color the beads on the sheet to make a color pattern instead. As children work, encourage them to describe the patterns.

Work closely with younger or less-confident learners and discuss the shape (or color) of each bead. Challenge older or more-confident learners to continue the patterns on their reproducible sheets.

Wrap-Up
Display page 7 of the Notebook file and explain that you will use the shapes provided to make some repeating patterns. Make the first pattern and ask children to describe it. Use the Undo button to reset the page. Invite a child to come to the SMART Board and make a pattern of their own choice. Discuss and describe the pattern together. Repeat this activity several times. Make a pattern—such as circle, square, circle, square, circle, square—by dragging and dropping shapes. Ask children to look at the pattern, then close their eyes. Insert another shape into the pattern. Invite children to open their eyes and look at the pattern. Ask: *Is this a pattern? What has happened to it?* Correct it by removing the additional shape.

Extending Patterns

Learning objectives
- Describe simple patterns involving shapes.
- Visualize and name common 2D shapes; use them to make patterns.

Resources
- "Extending Patterns" Notebook file
- beads and laces
- colored interlocking cubes
- pegs and pegboards
- colored counters
- digital camera

Whiteboard tools
- Pen tray
- Select tool
- Fill Color tool
- Screen Shade

Getting Started
Go to page 2 of the "Extending Patterns" Notebook file to reveal the first pattern of four shapes. Ask: *What should I put next? Why do you think so?* Drag on a square to duplicate it and drop it into position, and ask: *What is next?* Pull down the Screen Shade and repeat this for the next pattern.

Mini-Lesson
1. Go to page 3 of the Notebook file. Give children colored counters, and ask them to continue the pattern until they have used eight counters.

2. Say: *How would you describe this pattern? What comes next? And next? What colored circle should I put before the first one?* Together, add circles to the pattern on the board until there are eight altogether.

3. Reveal the second AABAAB pattern and repeat the activity.

4. Go to page 4. Tell children to look at the pattern carefully. Ask: *Is this pattern correct? What is wrong with it?* Invite them to suggest how it could be put right and fix the pattern. (You can use the Fill Color tool to change the shapes' color.)

5. Repeat this for the second AABAAB pattern.

Independent Work
Have children work in pairs. Provide each pair with a set of pattern-making materials. Ask children to begin a pattern. Then have them ask their partner to describe the pattern and continue it. If there are sufficient resources, they can keep their patterns to show during the Wrap-Up. Alternatively, take digital photographs and upload these to show during the Wrap-Up.

Begin patterns for less-confident learners to copy and continue. Challenge more-confident learners to make more complex patterns, including those that build up as well as across.

Wrap-Up
Invite a child to show his or her pattern to the class, or show a photograph of one that has been uploaded. Ask: *What is the pattern? How could you describe it? What would the next . . . and the next . . . and the next . . . [element] of the pattern be?* Repeat this for other children's work. Reveal the ABCABC pattern on page 5 of the Notebook file. Invite children to explain the pattern and say what comes next . . . and next . . . and to continue the pattern on the screen.

Find the Number

Learning objectives

- Solve problems involving counting, adding, subtracting, doubling, or halving in the context of measures.
- Describe ways of solving puzzles and problems, explaining choices and decisions orally.

Resources

- "Find the Number" Notebook file
- "How Shall I Solve It?" (p. 76)

Whiteboard tools

- Pen tray
- Select tool
- Highlighter pen

Getting Started

Display page 2 of the "Find the Number" Notebook file. Read aloud the question and ask children to figure out the answer. Write the number sentence 8 – 3 = 5 on the SMART Board. Ask a volunteer to explain how they found the answer. Ask: *Did anybody try a different way?* Discuss the different methods, if there are any, and their effectiveness. Go to page 3 and read the question. Discuss different solutions and write down the number sentence 8 + 2 = 10.

Mini-Lesson

1. Explain to children that in today's lesson they will be solving measuring problems. Go to page 4 of the "Find the Number" Notebook file and read aloud the problem.

2. Ask: *How can we work out the answer?* Invite children to say what the numbers are (4 and 2) and whether the number sentence to find the solution should be addition or subtraction. Invite a child to explain. Write 4 – 2 = 2 on the board.

3. Go to page 5 and read aloud the problem. Again, ask what the numbers are, and whether this is an addition or subtraction problem.

4. Ask: *How can you tell this is an addition problem?* Agree that the word *together* suggests addition, and highlight this word. Write the number sentence 7 + 5 = ___ on the board, and ask for the answer and the mental strategy used to figure this out.

Independent Work

Give out copies of "How Shall I Solve It?" (p. 76). Read through the problems together. Ask children to write a number sentence and then find the answer for each one.

Work with the less-confident learners as a group. Encourage them to explain how to solve each problem. Ask more-confident learners to write their own addition or subtraction problem for the Wrap-Up.

Wrap-Up

Review the problems and discuss how children solved them. Write the appropriate number sentences on page 6 of the Notebook file. Invite more-confident learners to read aloud their number problems. Challenge everybody to try to solve them.

What's Missing?

Learning objective
- Compare and order numbers, using the related vocabulary.

Resources
- "What's Missing?" Notebook file
- set of 0–20 numeral cards, one for each pair of children
- paper and pencils

Whiteboard tools
- Pen tray
- Select tool

Getting Started

Display the ten-space track on page 2 of the "What's Missing?" Notebook file. Write the number 1 at the beginning of the track and 10 at the end. Point to spaces and ask: *Which number fits here?* Ask children to help you write the numbers into the track. Then use the Eraser from the Pen tray to erase the numbers and repeat the activity for other starting numbers below 6.

Mini-Lesson

1. Reveal the 20-space number track on page 3 of the Notebook file.

2. Point to the space before 2 and ask: *Which number goes here?* Repeat this for other before and after numbers. Extend to other positions on the track until all the numbers are in place.

3. Leave the completed track on the SMART Board. Circle 6 and 9 and ask: *Which is more? Which is less? What numbers could fit between 6 and 9?* Agree that both 7 and 8 would fit.

4. Repeat this for other pairs of numbers, between 5 and 20. Encourage children to give a list of possible numbers.

Independent Work

Have children work in pairs. Provide each pair with a set of 0–20 numeral cards. Children should spread out the cards face-up on the table in front of them. Have them take turns choosing two numeral cards. They should then find a number that will fit between these two numbers. Ask children to record their numbers: the lower of the two card numbers, then the number that fits in between, and then the higher of the two card numbers.

Decide whether to limit the number range to up to 10, 12, or 15 for less-confident learners. Challenge more-confident learners to search for all the numbers that will fit between their chosen pairs of numbers.

Wrap-Up

Using the ten-space track on page 4 of the Notebook file, explain that you will write two numbers on the board. Challenge children to suggest all the numbers that will fit between these two. Begin with pairs of numbers with small differences, such as 7 and 11, or 9 and 13. Extend to pairs of numbers with larger differences, such as 3 and 12, or 5 and 14.

Clear the numbers on the track. Write into the central space the number 14. Challenge children to say the numbers that fit in the spaces that you point to, and write these in. Begin with either side of 14.

Function Machine

Learning objective
- Recall the doubles of all numbers to at least 10.

Resources
- "Function Machine" Notebook file
- 1-to-6 number cube for each pair of children
- paper and pencils
- blank number cube marked 4, 5, 6, 7, 8, 9 for more-confident learners

Whiteboard tools
- Pen tray
- Select tool
- Undo button

Getting Started

Explain to children that you are going to toss the on-screen number cube and that you want them to double the number that they see. Do this at a brisk pace so that children are encouraged to recall those double facts that they know. For those that they do not know, ask: *How could you figure this out?* Write in the boxes on page 2 of the "Function Machine" Notebook file to show the original and doubled numbers if children have difficulty with some numbers. Use the Eraser from the Pen tray to delete the written numbers and repeat the activity.

Mini-Lesson

1. Go to page 3 of the Notebook file. Explain that a number goes in on the left side of the function machine. The function machine then doubles it and adds 1. The answer comes out on the right side.

2. Ask children: *What would happen if we put 3 in the function machine?* Drag the number 3 through the machine; it will change to 7 when it exits the machine. Did children predict correctly?

3. Roll the on-screen number cube and write the number next to it. Ask: *What is double ___? And plus 1?* Write the answer on the right side.

4. Use the Undo button to erase the written numbers (or clear the page by selecting Edit, then Clear Page). Repeat the activity a few times.

5. When children are confident with this, repeat using the function "Double and subtract 1" on page 4. Again, drag the number 3 through the machine, asking children to predict the answer. Use the on-screen number cube to generate more numbers.

Independent Work

Have children work in pairs. Provide each pair with a number cube and paper and pencils for recording. Have partners take turns tossing the number cube and saying, "Double and add 1" or "Double and subtract 1." They both write a number sentence using the number from the cube (for example, 5 + 5 + 1 = ___, or 5 + 5 – 1 = ___) and write in their answers.

Decide whether or not to work with less-confident learners as a group. You may wish to limit their work to "Double and add 1." For more-confident learners, decide whether or not to provide number cubes with the numbers 4, 5, 6, 7, 8, 9.

Wrap-Up

Ask children to look at the number sentences that you are going to write on the SMART Board. Go to page 5 of the Notebook file. Point out the number sentence 5 + 6 in the first space on the left side of the screen. Ask: *How can we work this out?* Discuss the fact that 5 + 6 is the same as 5 + 5 + 1 and 6 + 6 – 1. Ask children to figure out the answer and to say which method they find easier and why. After writing children's suggestions in the top white box on the right-hand side of the page, pull the tab across to reveal how the answer can be worked out by splitting the numbers into "5 and a bit." Repeat the activity using other similar examples (for example, 6 + 7, 4 + 3, and so on). Decide whether to extend the range to up to 9 + 10 to challenge more-confident learners.

Comparing Lengths

Learning objective
- Estimate, measure, and compare objects, choosing and using suitable uniform nonstandard or standard units and measuring instruments (e.g., a yardstick).

Resources
- "Measuring" Notebook file
- craft materials
- nonstandard units for measuring, such as straws or cubes

Whiteboard tools
- Pen tray
- Screen Shade
- Select tool

Getting Started
Open page 2 of the "Measuring" Notebook file. Ask: *Which worm is longer? How can we find out?* Agree that the two images can be placed so that one of the ends is level with the other, and a direct comparison can be made. Repeat for the other pairs of images on pages 3 and 4.

Mini-Lesson
1. Enable the Screen Shade and go back to page 2 of the Notebook file. Reveal the first worm. Point out the squares on the right-hand side of the page, and ask: *How many squares long do you think the worm is?*

2. Drag and drop squares along the image to match its length. Agree how many squares were used, and write: ___ *squares long.*

3. Discuss how the squares may not exactly match the length or height of an image, and that vocabulary such as *almost* or *a bit over* can be used.

4. Repeat the activity to find out the length and height of the images on pages 3 and 4. Discuss how closely the squares match in length.

Independent Work
Have children work in mixed-ability groups of four. Provide each group with a set of craft materials and ask them to make some creatures. Provide some nonstandard units for measuring. Ask children to measure the length and height of their creatures. Children can record their creatures' length and height, and the units used, on a piece of paper that they place next to each creature. Ensure that each child is actively involved within his or her mixed-ability group and that the more-confident learners do not dominate the work of the group.

Wrap-Up
Invite children to order their creatures by length, shortest first. Remind them to keep the record of length and height by each creature. Ask: *Which is the longest? How long is that? So which is the shortest? What did that measure?* Challenge children to describe a creature, in the form of ___ *is longer than* ___ *but shorter than* ___. Repeat this for height.

   Now ask children to decide whether the order would be the same if the creatures were reordered by height. Ask: *How would you measure the width of each creature?* Measure the widths and reorder the creatures, narrowest first. Ask children to describe the position of their creatures in the row, in the form of ___ *is wider than* ___ *but narrower than* ___. Repeat this activity using page 5 of the Notebook file. Ask for volunteers to order the animals by length, measuring as required.

Ordering by Size

Learning objectives

- Order two or three items by length or height.
- Use developing mathematical ideas and methods to solve practical problems.

Resources

- prepared Notebook file (see Before You Start)
- play dough, boards, and tools
- 2D shape tiles
- "Sizing Up Animals" (p. 77)

Whiteboard tools

- Shapes tool
- Select tool

Before You Start

Prepare a Notebook file as follows:

- Page 1 — insert a 2D shape
- Pages 2 and onward — a page of 2D shapes, such as three triangles that are each a different size (make sure the shapes are not in size order). Prepare additional pages, using other shapes, and increase the number of shapes to be ordered to four or five for the Wrap-Up activity.

Getting Started

Distribute the shape tiles among children. Open the first page of your prepared Notebook file (see Before You Start). Ask children to sort their shape tiles and to find the shape displayed on the SMART Board. Invite them to take turns naming the shape and telling you one of its properties.

Mini-Lesson

1. Reveal the first set of three shapes on page 2 of the Notebook file. Ask: *What are these shapes? Are they all the same? What is different about them?* Discuss the different sizes of the shapes and how children know which is the smallest and which is the largest.

2. Ask children to tell you which is the smallest shape. Place this one first, on the left side of the page. Now ask: *Which is the largest shape?* Place this to the right side of the page. Ask: *Where does the remaining shape go?* Place this in the middle of the other two.

3. Discuss how the shapes are in size order, from smallest to largest. Ask: *How can we move the shapes around so that the largest is first?* Follow children's suggestions, moving the shapes so that they are now ordered with the largest first.

4. Repeat for the other shapes on your subsequent Notebook pages.

Independent Work

Arrange for an adult to work with a group of four to six children. (Repeat this activity during the week so that each group has time to work with an adult.) Each child will need some play dough, a board, and some tools. Invite children to make a shape like the first animal on the reproducible "Sizing Up Animals" (p. 77). Ask children to make another animal, but this time larger. Repeat for one larger still. Now invite children to order their animals, smallest first, then largest first. Ask children to describe the shapes of their animals, including their sizes.

This activity is accessible for all ability levels. Help younger or less-confident learners with mathematical vocabulary and challenge older or more-confident learners to be more explicit in their descriptions.

Wrap-Up

Display your prepared Notebook page showing four shapes of different sizes. Invite children to describe each shape, including its size. Ask children to help you order these, smallest first. Repeat, this time ordering the shapes with the largest first.

Units of Measurement

Getting Started

Open page 2 of the "Measuring" Notebook file. Ask children to say which of the two worms is longer, shorter, wider, narrower, and how they know this. Repeat for the other pairs of items on pages 3 and 4.

Mini-Lesson

1. Enable the Screen Shade and go back to page 2 of the Notebook file. Reveal one of the images.

2. Explain that you would like children to decide which of the units on screen would be suitable for measuring the worm. Ask: *How long do you estimate the worm to be?* Write down some of the estimates.

3. Now drag and drop the chosen unit along the worm. Ask: *Was this a good choice of unit? Why do you think that? Did you make a good guess?*

4. Repeat this for other items on pages 2, 3, and 4 of the Notebook file, each time asking children to choose the appropriate units.

5. Encourage them to use the vocabulary of approximation in their answers, such as *about, and a bit,* and *almost.*

Independent Work

Have children work in mixed-ability groups of four. Provide each group with sets of nonstandard units, so that they need to make a choice about the appropriate unit, and sets of things to measure. Ask children to take turns choosing something to measure and deciding which unit they will use to measure it. They should each make an estimate first, then measure and record their results. They can record their results in a simple table. For example:

I chose a...	My units are...	My estimate is...	My measure is...

Check that the more-confident learners do not dominate the groups. Take time to discuss with the less-confident learners the choices they make.

Wrap-Up

Go to page 6 of the Notebook file, which shows a selection of measuring units. Draw a thick line on the page. Ask: *Which units shall we use to measure this line? How long do you think it is?* Drag and drop units along the line. Agree on a measurement, using vocabulary such as *about* or *and a bit.*

Learning objective

- Estimate, measure, and compare objects, choosing and using suitable uniform nonstandard or standard units and measuring instruments (e.g., a yardstick).

Resources

- "Measuring" Notebook file
- sets of uniform nonstandard units
- items that can be measured (for example, small toys, pencils, brushes)
- paper and pencils
- strips of paper
- scissors

Whiteboard tools

- Pen tray
- Screen Shade
- Select tool

Telling Time

Learning objective
- Read the time to the hour and half hour.

Resources
- "Telling Time" Notebook file
- "What Time Is It?" (p. 78), copied onto cardstock and cut apart, for each pair of children (You may wish to write the correct time on the back of each card, if children are not confident with telling the time.)
- teaching clock face
- individual clock faces, one for each child

Whiteboard tools
- Pen tray
- Select tool

Getting Started

Open page 2 of the "Telling Time" Notebook file. Look at the clock faces, and agree that all of them show o'clock times. Ask children to set their individual clock faces to the first time and to show you. Together, say what time that is. Repeat this for the other times shown on pages 3 to 6. Invite a child to remove each box to reveal the correct time.

Mini-Lesson

1. Use the teaching clock to show children how the clock hands are set for 2:30. Say: *This clock shows half past two. The minute hand is pointing to the six, so that we know it is a half-past time.* Elicit from children that the hour hand is pointing to midway between the 2 and the 3.

2. Go to page 7 of the Notebook file. Again, ask children to set their individual clock faces to match this set of clocks. For each time, check that children set their clocks accurately and can say the time. Remove the boxes to reveal the correct time.

3. Invite a child to describe the position of the hands for each half-past time.

4. Repeat the activity on pages 8 to 11.

Independent Work

Give each pair of children a set of cards made from "What Time Is It?" (p. 78) and ask them to shuffle the pack. (Give less-confident learners cards with the correct times written on the back.) Have children take turns taking a card and asking their partner to say the time on the card. They repeat this until all the cards have been used. Then challenge children to order the clock times starting with 1:00.

Provide less-confident learners with individual clock faces. Ask children to set their clock face to each time shown on the cards, as well as reading the times. Challenge more-confident learners to choose some times that are important to them, and to be ready to say during the Wrap-Up what they do at these times. This could include the time they get up, leave home in the morning, or go to bed at night.

Wrap-Up

Go to page 12 of the Notebook file. Repeat the activity from Getting Started. Note that these are a mixture of o'clock and half-past times. Repeat the activity on pages 13 to 16. Invite more-confident learners to say one of their times and talk about why it is important to them. Ask the other children to set their clocks to this time.

Collecting Data

Learning objectives
- Answer a question by recording information in lists and tables.
- Present outcomes using practical resources, pictures, and bar graphs.

Resources
- "Collecting Data" Notebook file
- different items collected on a science nature walk (e.g., leaves, stones, and twigs)
- paper plates
- small squares of sticky notes
- large sheets of construction paper
- a collection of items that can be sorted in more than one way (for example, different colored shapes that can be sorted by shape or by color)

Whiteboard tools
- Pen tray
- Select tool
- Area Capture tool

Getting Started
Open page 2 of the "Collecting Data" Notebook file. Ask children to name the days of the week and make a note of them. Discuss how it is helpful to make lists when collecting information. Ask: *What are the days of the week? How many have the same ending?* (All of them) *How many begin with the same letter?* (Two with *S*, two with *T*) Make lists of the information on the SMART Board. Repeat for other types of information.

Mini-Lesson
1. Divide the class into small groups. Provide each group with paper plates and items collected on the nature walk (see Resources). Ask each group to sort the items.

2. Go to page 3 of the Notebook file. Ask: *How did you sort your items?* Check that children have sorted them correctly (for example, into leaves, stones, and so on).

3. Use page 3 to make notes on how the sets of items can be combined (for example, all the plates of leaves, all the plates of stones). Give each group one set of items to count and ask them to write down the result.

4. Go to page 4. Explain to children that they are going to make a bar graph to show how many there are of each type of item.

5. Invite each group to say what items they counted. Use these items as labels for each column and type them in the boxes (for example, *Leaves*, *Twigs*). Now drag and drop a block for each item counted. Discuss how the blocks fit together so that it is possible to see, without counting, which set has more items and which has fewer. Agree on a title for the bar graph and type it in the box..

6. Ask questions about the data, such as: *Are there more leaves or more twigs? Which set has the most items? Which set has fewer than five items?*

7. Use the Area Capture tool to take a snapshot of the completed bar graph.

Independent Work
Divide the class into mixed-ability groups of about four. Give each group a collection of items to sort, paper plates, a large sheet of construction paper, and small squares of sticky notes. Ask children to sort their items onto the paper plates. They should then write headings for the columns of the bar graph, and stick a square of paper for each item in the correct column. They can then decide on and write a title for the graph. Challenge them to find a different way to sort the items and repeat the activity.

Ensure that each child is actively involved within his or her mixed-ability group and that the more-confident learners do not dominate the work of the group. As children work, invite them to explain how they decided to sort and why.

Wrap-Up
Look at some of the children's graphs. Ask questions such as: *Which set has the most items? Which has the fewest items? How can you tell? Which has more/fewer than ___?* Ask for volunteers to produce their graphs using page 5 of the Notebook file.

2D Shapes

Learning objectives

- Begin to use mathematical names for flat 2D shapes and mathematical terms to describe shapes.
- Use language such as *circle* or *bigger* to describe the shape and size of solids and flat shapes.

Resources

- "2D Shapes" Notebook file
- tile sets of squares, circles, stars, triangles, and rectangles

Whiteboard tools

- Pen tray
- Select tool
- Spotlight tool
- Undo button

Getting Started

Distribute the tile shapes among children. Display the triangle on page 2 of the "2D Shapes" Notebook file. Ask children to sort the shapes in front of them to find the shape that they see. Ask: *What is this shape called?* Agree that it is a triangle. Select the shape and rotate it (by pressing and dragging the green circle) to change its orientation. Ask children to decide whether or not it is the same shape. Activate the Spotlight tool before moving to the next page of the Notebook file.

Mini-Lesson

1. Invite children to work in groups, with a box of 2D shapes in front of them.

2. Explain that you will think of a shape and describe it. Children must listen to your clues and sort out the shapes in front of them, putting back into the box, one at a time, any that do not fit the description.

3. Give the first clue, revealing a little of the square on page 3 with the spotlight. Keep giving clues and providing glimpses of the shape until children have found the shape that you are thinking of. You could say, for example: *My shape has four sides. All the sides are the same length.*

4. When children have guessed, turn off the Spotlight tool to reveal your shape.

5. Repeat for the circle on page 4. Say, for example: *My shape is curved. It has just one line, which goes all around my shape.*

6. Children may use everyday language to name shapes such as *round* instead of *circle*. Introduce the mathematical names, but accept the more familiar names at this stage. Make sure, however, that children do not confuse the names of 3D and 2D shapes, such as *square* versus *cube* or *box*.

Independent Work

Go to page 5 of the Notebook file and show children the house made from shapes. Ask them to help you copy the picture by directing you as you move the shapes provided into place. Once you have completed the picture, press the Undo button until the page is reset. Invite volunteers to come to the SMART Board and try to make the house shape themselves.

Next, provide pairs of children with some tile shapes. Invite them to choose some shapes to make a picture of their own choice, such as a face, an animal, a house, and so on. As children work, encourage them to name and describe the shapes that they choose. Encourage them to use mathematical vocabulary as they describe their shapes.

Support younger or less-confident learners by providing ideas of pictures to create. Challenge older or more-confident learners to be more explicit in their descriptions.

Wrap-Up

Go to page 6 of the Notebook file. Ask children to look in their boxes of shapes to find the shapes that they can see on the screen. Invite volunteers to use the shapes to create a picture of their own choice on the Notebook page.

More Shapes

Learning objective

- Visualize and name common 2D shapes and 3D solids and describe their features.

Resources

- "More Shapes" Notebook file
- 2D shape tiles
- assorted 3D shapes
- drawing materials

Whiteboard tools

- Pen tray
- Spotlight tool
- Fill Color tool
- Highlighter pen
- Select tool

Getting Started

Open the "More Shapes" Notebook file, enable the Spotlight tool, and go to page 2. Show a triangle and ask: *What is this shape called?* Repeat this for the other 2D shapes. Then disable the Spotlight tool and use the Fill Color tool to change the color of each shape to black to reveal its name, to check if children's answers were correct. Enable the Spotlight again, turn to page 3 and repeat the activity, this time using the Eraser from the Pen tray to reveal the answers.

Mini-Lesson

1. Provide each group with a set of 2D and 3D shapes.

2. Say: *I am thinking of a shape. It has straight sides. What shape could I be thinking of?* Encourage children to sort the shapes.

3. Go back to page 2 of the Notebook file. Ask for volunteers to sort the shapes with straight sides from the other shapes.

4. Say: *My shape has three sides.* Agree that this is a triangle. Point out a triangle on page 2 and discuss its properties.

5. Ask for volunteers to group all the triangles together.

6. Go to page 4. Say: *Discuss this shape with the others in your group. Make a sentence to describe something about this shape.* Ask for responses. Write children's sentences in the space provided.

7. Repeat this for pages 5 to 7.

8. Go back to page 3. Discuss 3D shapes, pointing out that these shapes have faces that are 2D shapes, such as squares and triangles. Highlight and label the 2D shape faces.

Independent Work

Provide each group with drawing materials. Ask children to choose a 3D shape and to draw each of its faces. Children should write the names of the faces of their shapes. Display page 3 of the Notebook file on the SMART Board to provide vocabulary. Children should write a sentence for each of their 3D shapes, describing one of its properties.

Decide whether or not to work with less-confident learners as a group. Encourage them to use and understand the vocabulary of shape. Challenge more-confident learners to write more than one sentence to describe each shape.

Wrap-Up

Point to one of the 3D shapes on page 8 of the Notebook file. Ask: *What faces does this shape have?* Use a Highlighter pen to highlight the 2D shapes in the 3D shapes. Drag the appropriate 2D shape at the foot of the page and drop it under the 3D shape. Ask: *What sentence can you say to describe this shape?* Write a good example under the shape. Repeat this for the other shapes.

What's in a Shape?

earning objectives

• Describe simple patterns and relationships involving shapes; decide whether examples satisfy given conditions.

• Describe ways of solving puzzles and problems, explaining choices and decisions orally.

Resources

• "What's in a Shape?" Notebook file
• individual whiteboards and pens
• sets of assorted 2D shapes (including different examples of squares, rectangles, and triangles), one set for each group of four to six children
• large piece of paper and pencils for recording

Whiteboard tools

• Pen tray
• Spotlight tool
• Select tool

Getting Started

Open page 2 of the "What's in a Shape?" Notebook file. Enable the Spotlight tool and focus on one of the shapes. Ask children to name the shape and ask questions about its properties. For example, for a triangle, children might say it has three straight sides and three angles. Repeat for other 2D shapes on page 2, and for 3D shapes on page 3.

Mini-Lesson

1. Provide each child with an individual whiteboard and pen.

2. Spotlight a triangle on page 2 of the Notebook file. Say: *All triangles have three sides. Is this true?* Ask children to draw a triangle and to hold up their whiteboards when you say *Show me*. Check that everyone has drawn a triangle.

3. Now invite children to look at others' drawings. Ask: *Do all triangles have three sides?*

4. Go to page 4 of the Notebook file, so that children can see a right, scalene, equilateral, and isosceles triangle. Agree that all the triangles have the same number of sides. Ask: *What else do triangles have?* Agree that they all have straight sides and three angles. Write this on the SMART Board.

5. Repeat this activity for the circles on page 5.

Independent Work

Explain that you would like children to find examples for these statements:

• All rectangles have four straight sides.

• All circles have a curved side.

• All triangles have three angles.

In groups of four to six, children should sort the 2D shapes on their table. They can record by choosing the appropriate shapes and drawing around them on paper.

Decide whether or not to work with less-confident learners as a group. Encourage them to use the vocabulary of shape to describe the shapes they sort, focusing on how these are the same or different. Challenge more-confident learners to find an example for this statement: *All the squares of the same size fit together, leaving no gaps.*

Wrap-Up

Invite children from each ability group to show examples of their work to the rest of the class. Ask them to explain how their shapes fit the statement. Go to page 6 of the Notebook file. Ask: *What are these? What sentence can you say that tells me about these shapes?* Agree that all rectangles have four straight sides. Discuss how rectangles have opposite sides of the same length. Go back to page 2 and ask for volunteers to sort the shapes into triangles, rectangles, circles, and squares. Over time, repeat this work for 3D shapes.

Making Models

Learning objective
- Visualize and name common 2D shapes and 3D solids and describe their features; use them to make models.

Resources
- "Making Models" Notebook file
- a collection of 3D shapes for each group of children
- paper, pencils, and drawing materials
- printouts of page 5 of the Notebook file, one for each child

Whiteboard tools
- Pen tray
- Select tool
- Gallery

Getting Started
Open page 2 of the "Making Models" Notebook file. Divide the class into small groups and give each group an assortment of 3D shapes. They should sort the shapes, find the cube, and name it. Ask: *How many faces does it have? What shape are they? How could you describe a cube to someone else?* Repeat this for other shapes in their collections.

Mini-Lesson
1. Go to page 3 of the Notebook file. Invite children to make the model with real cubes.
2. Ask: *How many cubes are there? What shape have you made?* (A tower)
3. Take the on-screen tower apart and invite a volunteer to build it again.
4. Use the shapes on page 4 to build a simple model. Then invite children to build the model with their shapes. Ask: *How do these shapes fit together?*
5. Repeat, making the model more complex.
6. Give out paper and pencils. Make a simple model on the SMART Board and ask children to make a sketch of what they see.
7. Deconstruct the on-screen model. Ask children to swap drawings with a partner, and then build the model using their partner's drawing. Invite them to discuss how easy this was and how the drawings could be improved.
8. Invite a volunteer to rebuild the model on the Notebook page.

Independent Work
Display page 5 of the Notebook file. Provide each child with a printout of the page, paper, and drawing materials, together with some 3D shapes for building. In small mixed-ability groups, each child should make his or her own model, and then compare it with the printout and with the models of the other members of the group.

Next, ask children to create their own model and to draw it on a piece of paper. Ask them to choose models from their group that they think are accurately made. These will be used in the Wrap-Up. Ensure that each child is actively involved within his or her mixed-ability group and that the more-confident learners do not dominate the work of the group.

Wrap-Up
Scan some children's drawings of models and display them. Compare two models that depict the same drawing. Ask: *How are these the same as the drawing? How are they different?* Encourage the use of shape vocabulary. Repeat this for other models. Invite children to suggest some 3D shapes that could be dragged and dropped onto the screen to make a model. Obtain some 3D shapes from the Gallery and place them on page 6 of the Notebook file. Give children a few minutes to make a model using real versions of these shapes. Compare their models with the one on the Notebook page.

Mazes

Learning objective

- Visualize and use everyday language to describe the position of objects and the direction and distance when moving them, for example when placing or moving objects on a game board.

Resources

- "Mazes" Notebook file
- "Animal Homes" (p. 79)

Whiteboard tools

- Pen tray
- Select tool
- Highlighter pen

Getting Started

Carry out this activity in a space where children can move freely. Say: *I am going to give you some instructions for moving and turning. Listen carefully, then follow the instructions.* Begin with simple, one-move instructions, such as: *Turn right; turn left; take one step forward/back.* When children are confident with this, give more complex instructions that involve two actions, such as: *Move forward three steps then turn right.* If children are unsure of which is their left or right side, consider giving them something to hold in their right hand so that they can identify this side of themselves with ease.

Mini-Lesson

1. Go to page 2 of the "Mazes" Notebook file. Ask children to look carefully at the maze. Explain that you would like them to decide how to move the child (in the bottom left-hand corner) from home to the school. Invite them to give directions for doing this.

2. Children will not be able to give a specific distance instruction, but should be able to say, for example: *Move forward; turn right/left at the bend.* Use a Highlighter pen to highlight the route according to their instructions. Then move the child to the final place following the route (or invite a child to do so).

3. Invite children to give other suggestions for moving the child from home to school.

4. Repeat this for other moves between two points on the Notebook page.

Independent Work

Have children work in pairs and provide each pair with a copy of "Animal Homes" (p. 79). Tell them to take turns deciding which animal is to go home. Have each partner find and describe a route for the animal to get home. When they have sent all the animals home, they should decide on another animal, draw the animal and its home on the sheet, and then find a way for their animal to get home.

Decide whether or not to work with less-confident learners as a group. Help them develop the vocabulary of position and movement. Challenge more-confident learners to give instructions for visiting each home in turn.

Wrap-Up

Go to page 3 of the Notebook file and ask children to give instructions for moving between any two attractions at the zoo. Invite children to choose two types of animals to visit. They should devise routes to those animals and describe the routes to their neighbor, to practice describing the routes to the class. Ask some children to describe their routes. Follow the routes with a Highlighter pen and ask the other children if they agree with the chosen routes. Finally, tell children that the zoo will be closing soon. Ask them to describe the routes they will take to the parking lot.

Counting Mat

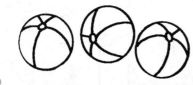   

Ten in the Bed

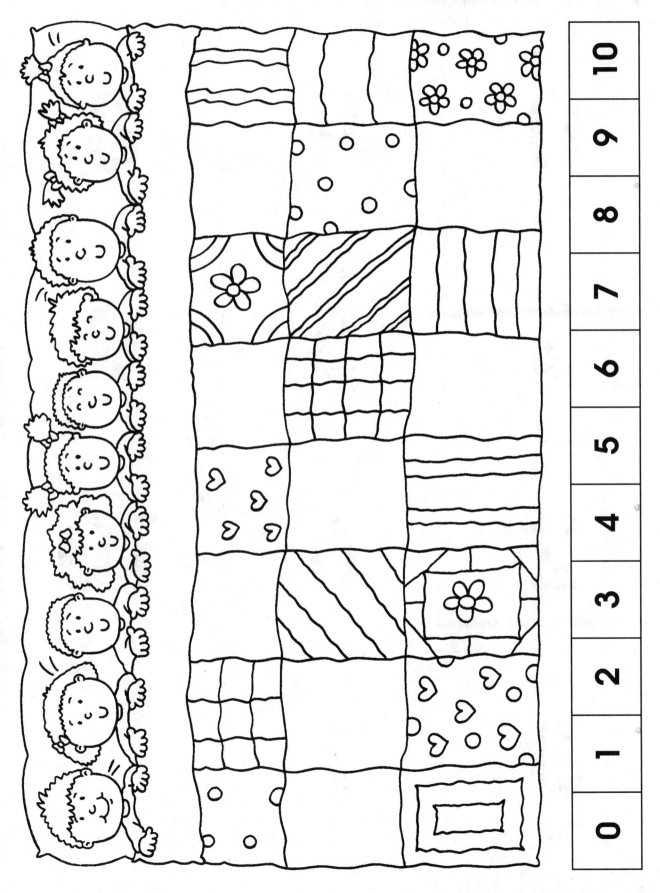

Numerals

0	4	8
1	5	9
2	6	10
3	7	

Recording How Many

Draw some marks to match the number.

1	
2	
3	
4	
5	
6	

Count and Write the Numerals

Take turns with your partner to take some counting toys. Count and draw the toys. Write how many there are.

Number	Draw the toys

Which Is First

Make each car a different color. What color is the first car?

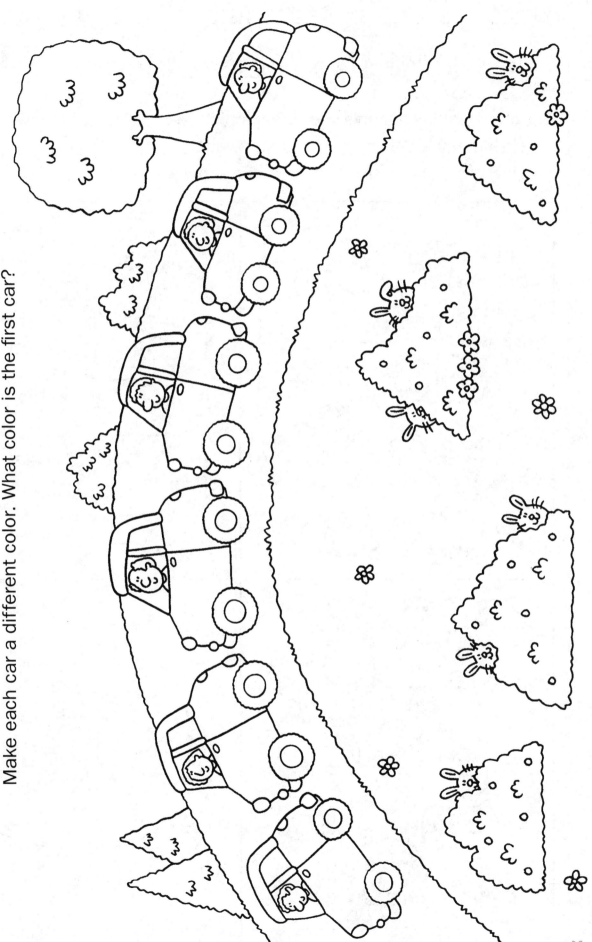

Solve the Problems

Count how many animals are in each picture.

- How many are there if one goes away?
- How many are there if another one arrives?

Two Sets

Three Sets

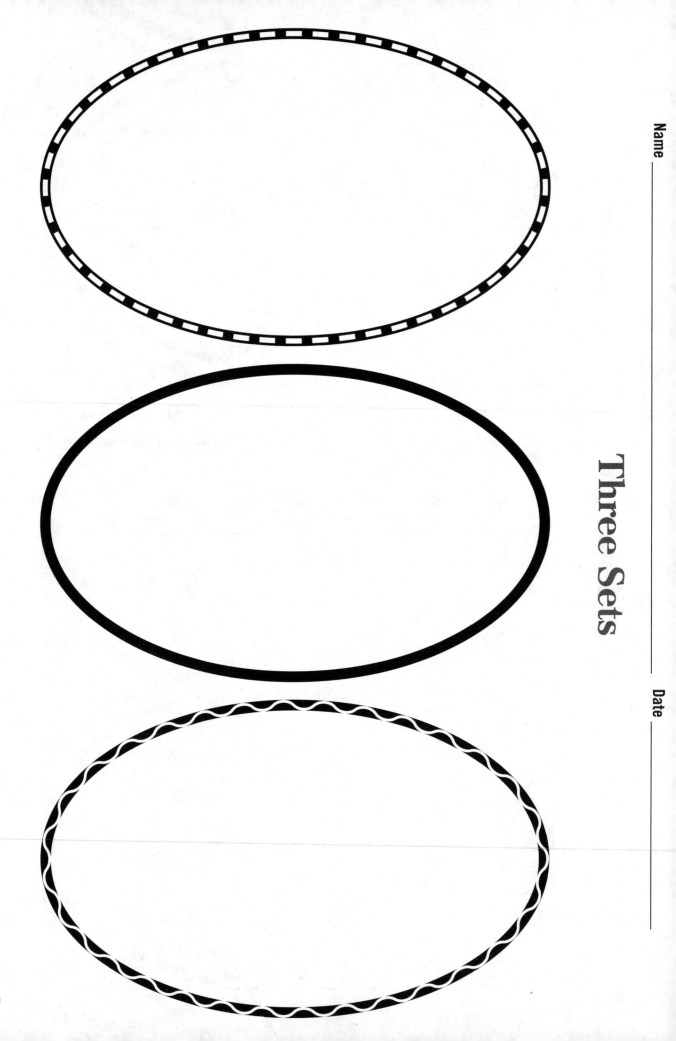

Making Totals

Find two sets of animals that make a total of six. Place matching counters on each pair of sets.

How Many More?

Read each problem to the children. Ask them to solve it by counting up from the lower to the higher number.

1. There are four ducks on the pond. There are six chickens in the barn. How many more chickens than ducks are there?

2. There are seven raisins in Molly's lunchbox. There are four raisins in Peter's lunchbox. Who has more? How many more?

3. There are four apples on the plate. Eight children would like an apple. How many more apples do we need?

4. There are seven dogs. There are only three kennels. But every dog would like a kennel. How many more kennels do we need?

5. Nine cats are hungry. There are only six bowls of cat food. How many more bowls of cat food do we need?

6. Eight children want to play in the snow. There are only six pairs of mittens. How many more pairs of mittens do we need?

7. There are four bowls of ice cream. Ten children would like some ice cream. How many more bowls of ice cream do we need?

8. Nine children want to paint a picture. There are only two easels. How many more easels do we need?

Larger Number First

You will need:
- A 1-to-6 number cube
- A set of 1-to-4 numeral cards

Work with a partner.
- Take turns throwing the cube and choosing a number card.
- Use the two numbers to write an addition sentence.
  Remember to put the larger number first.
- Write the total.

Dice	Card	Addition sentence (larger number first)	Total

Writing Addition Sentences

Here are eight fish. Find different ways to put eight fish into two circles.

Record each way you find by drawing the fish into the circles below. Write an addition sentence to show what you have done.

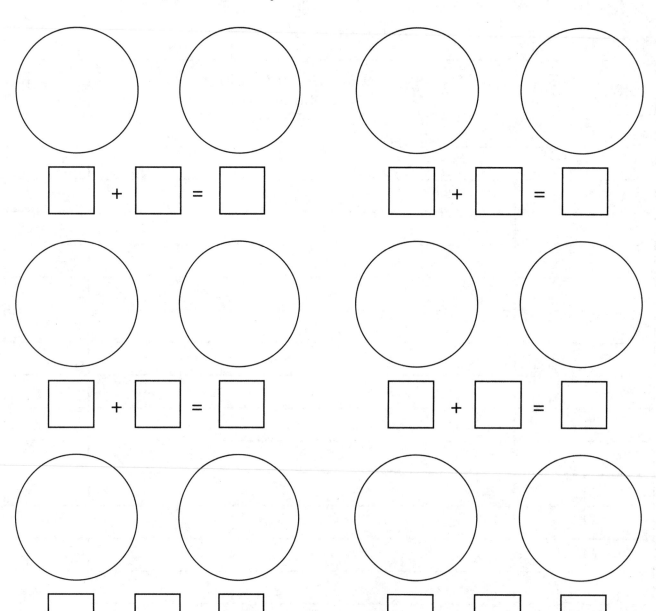

Digit Cards

1 0   2 0   3 0

0   1   2   3

4   5   6

7   8   9

69

Splitting Numbers

Work with a partner.

- Take turns choosing two numbers on the grid.
- Write a number sentence and figure out the answer.
- The other player checks the answer.
- Cross out the numbers you chose.

6	6	6
7	7	7
8	8	8
9	9	9

Player 1

$5 + \boxed{} + 5 + \boxed{} = 10 + \boxed{} = \boxed{}$

$5 + \boxed{} + 5 + \boxed{} = 10 + \boxed{} = \boxed{}$

$5 + \boxed{} + 5 + \boxed{} = 10 + \boxed{} = \boxed{}$

Player 2

$5 + \boxed{} + 5 + \boxed{} = 10 + \boxed{} = \boxed{}$

$5 + \boxed{} + 5 + \boxed{} = 10 + \boxed{} = \boxed{}$

$5 + \boxed{} + 5 + \boxed{} = 10 + \boxed{} = \boxed{}$

Make a Ten

Work with a partner.

- Take turns choosing two numbers from the box.
- Write a number sentence.
- Both of you work out the answer.
- Repeat this until you have eight different number sentences.

6	7	8	9

_____ + _____ = _____

_____ + _____ = _____

_____ + _____ = _____

_____ + _____ = _____

_____ + _____ = _____

_____ + _____ = _____

_____ + _____ = _____

_____ + _____ = _____

Counting Coins

Work in pairs.

1. You need a 1-to-6 number cube and some pennies.

2. Take turns rolling the cube.

3. Take that number of pennies and put them onto the stars.

4. The first person to collect 10 pennies wins the game!

Name _____

Name _____

What Fits?

Work with a partner.

1. You will each need a colored crayon and a counter.

2. Take turns putting a counter on an empty square on the number track.

3. Ask your partner to say what number belongs in this square.

4. If you both agree, then your partner writes in the number.

5. Repeat until all the numbers are written onto the track.

Number Tracks

1. Write in the missing numbers.

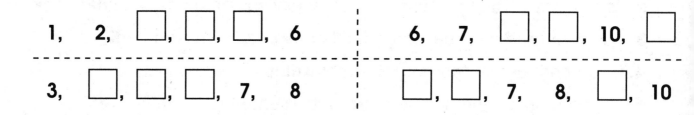

1,   2,   ☐, ☐, ☐,   6   ⋮   6,   7,   ☐, ☐, 10, ☐

3,   ☐, ☐, ☐,   7,   8   ⋮   ☐, ☐,   7,   8,   ☐, 10

2. Write where these numbers will fit on the track.

5 9 2 4

1									10

11   6   8   7

3									12

12   10   7   14

6									15

3. Write the numbers from 1 to 20 in this track.

1									10

4. Write in the missing numbers on these tracks.

		6					12	
	7						13	

Follow the Patterns

You will need beads and laces. Make the patterns. Continue the patterns.

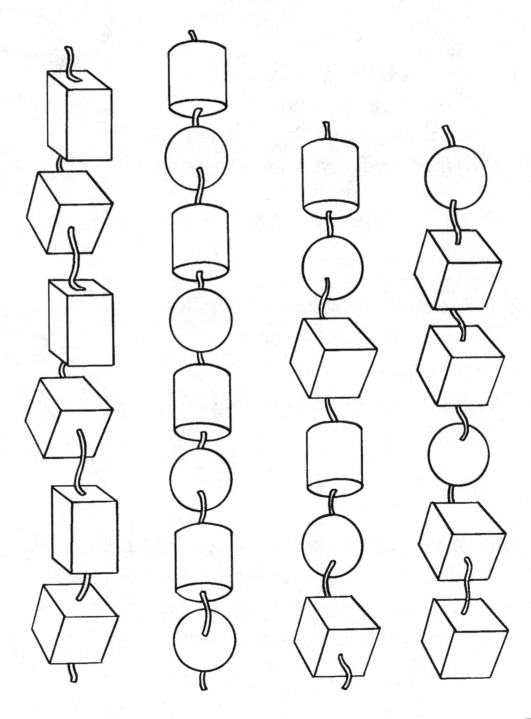

How Shall I Solve It?

Read each problem. Write a number sentence. Write the answer.

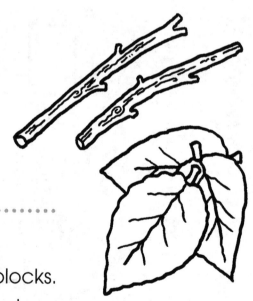

1. Paul collects some rocks.

   There are six rocks in one box.

   There are eight rocks in the other box.

   How many rocks are there altogether?

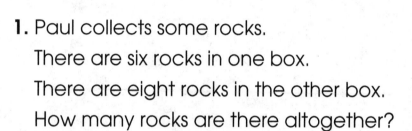

2. Jody collects two sticks.

   One stick is four inches long.

   The other stick is nine inches long.

   How long are the two sticks in total?

3. Sarah balances all her leaves with 12 blocks.

   She put some of her leaves on to the balance.

   These leaves balance with seven blocks.

   How many blocks will balance the rest of Sarah's leaves?

Sizing Up Animals

Make these animals.

What Time Is It?

Animal Homes

Work with a partner.

1. Take turns choosing an animal and its home.

2. Now ask your partner to tell you how the animal could get home.

Think of another animal.

1. Draw it on the maze.

2. Now draw its home.

3. Find a way for the animal to get home.

Notes